Wallace Arnold Days

Wallace Arnold

N218 HWX

Wallace Arnold

8332 U

Allan
PUBLISHING

Roger Davies and Stephen Barber

Front cover: WA dealt in pairs — good drivers and smart coaches, Plaxton and Volvo, all summed up by this superb shot taken looking over Scarborough. All aboard for *Wallace Arnold Days!* *Plaxton / Stephen Barber collection*

Back cover: The showroom at Plaxton's Scarborough plant witnessed many WA handover celebrations. This view was recorded in 1993, when the relationship between WA and Plaxton was at its lowest ebb following the disaster with the 1992 deliveries, and these three coaches represent 60% of the Plaxton order, the remaining order for 45 coaches having been placed with Van Hool and Jonckheere. But Plaxton was to bounce back, and history shows the 60-year relationship between the leaders in their respective industries was special. *Plaxton / Stephen Barber collection*

Previous page: Almost 40 years of Plaxton progress, but still the same old British weather. In 1996 a newly delivered Volvo B10M/Plaxton Premiere, N218 HWX, poses for photographs alongside preserved AEC Reliance 8332 U dating from 1958. *Stewart J. Brown*

Right: One of the 1963 Plaxton-bodied Leyland Leopards stands outside London's Victoria station, awaiting its passengers while on tour. To attempt this today would likely bring the centre of the capital to a standstill. *Stephen Barber collection*

First published 2010

ISBN 978 0 7110 3438 9

© Ian Allan Publishing Ltd 2010

Published by Ian Allan Publishing

an imprint of Ian Allan Publishing Ltd, Hersham, Surrey, KT12 4RG

Printed in England by Ian Allan Printing Ltd, Hersham, Surrey, KT12 4RG

Distributed in Canada and the United States of America by BookMasters Distribution Services

Code: 1005/X

Visit the Ian Allan Publishing website at www.ianallanpublishing.com

ITINERARY

Acknowledgements

Many photographs and artefacts reproduced in this book are from the collections of Stephen Barber and Stuart Jones. Unfortunately the origin of some of the photographs is unknown; in each case every effort has been made to establish the copyright-holder, and to any we have missed we offer sincere apologies. Much of this book is made up of personal reminiscences, and to the following we owe a deep debt of gratitude. So sincere thanks to John King, Geoffrey Steel, Barbara Flin, Reg Hele, Major Elphee, John Fisher, Paul Haywood, Alan Millar, Ray Stenning, Andrew Braddock, Andrew Wiltshire, Perry Cliff, the *Yorkshire Evening Post*, Tom Cobbleigh and all. Special mention, as ever, goes to the late John Cockshot, who took so many excellent WA shots over the years. The fleet histories of the PSV Circle and Ian Allan's *British Bus Fleets No 9* were also most helpful, as was *Holidays by Coach*, by Stewart J. Brown.

FOREWORD

'This is not a definitive history' is a phrase frequently bandied about in books like this that are based on … er … history. However, the detailed history of the famous Wallace Arnold company can be found in *Glory Days: Wallace Arnold*, and we don't intend to repeat it here. Yes, you will, inevitably, get the gist of it in the following pages, and we have developed the tale of the later years more fully. But in essence this book tries to bring out in words and pictures what the company was like, what it did, and some of the characters who made it. So take your seats please — we are on our way.

Roger Davies
Stephen Barber
March 2010

Right: WA was always proud of its fleet and was not afraid to remind people of the scale of investment needed to keep it at the forefront of the industry. This PR shot features an awkwardly posed Stephen Barber welcoming new arrivals to Gelderd Road as Graham Stirk, at the wheel of Volvo B10M/ Plaxton Première N202 HWX, gives the thumbs-up. The coaches are the first wave of the 1996 order of 51, worth over £7 million.
Stephen Barber collection

As usual, on the evening of 31 March 2005, Wallace Arnold's coaches finished their day's work. As usual, they were cleaned ready for duty the next day. But this was no usual night — this was the *last* night. When the coaches rolled out the following day — April Fools' Day — they were Shearings coaches. For a while there was a nod towards WA identity, but within an indecently short time a major element of the UK's travel scene was gone forever.

So how did this come about? To find out we need to take a trip — a tour, if you will — back in time.

Above: Gelderd Road in 1995, showing the make-up of the fleet, different rear-end designs and provision for passengers. Three Van Hools, three Jonckheeres and two Plaxtons are in evidence. *Stephen Barber collection*

Let us begin by introducing the company's founder, Robert Barr. He had grown up in the countryside on his parents' farm at Woolley, near Wakefield, and, horrified by the conditions he saw in West Riding towns, formulated a vision for providing the opportunity for town folk to enjoy the countryside he loved so much. Moving to Leeds in 1904, he obtained a job at Bridge Street Garage in Lower Briggate, as he was fascinated by things mechanical — something that often brought him into conflict with his traditionally minded father. He worked hard, doing overtime and additional jobs in such spare time he had, and in 1912 bought his first vehicle, a Karrier, to start excursions into the Dales at weekends whilst running a lorry business during the week. The firm, R. Barr (Leeds), grew but was drastically reduced during World War 1.

After the war Robert set about rebuilding his company and as early as 1920 was running a trip from Leeds to London — quite a feat, given the then top speed of 12mph. In 1926, seeking to broaden his horizons, he had a meeting in Leeds with two gentlemen — Messrs Wallace Cunningham and Arnold Crowe — and paid them £800 for their established charabanc business, which already offered tours to London, Edinburgh and the Highlands. He decided that his own name should continue to apply to his existing lorry business but that the coaching operation should retain the names of its previous owners.

Soon Wallace Arnold coaches were at the forefront of most developments, moving from charabancs to all-weather coaches by 1928 and to all-rubber-tyred vehicles, which turned out to be a very useful development when the speed limit for vehicles fitted with pneumatic tyres was raised from 12 to 20mph. However, Robert Barr's original vision of providing affordable travel for the masses wasn't exactly realised, as WA tours were very much the preserve of the middle class, to high-class hotels — from 1933 including Continental destinations — using top-of-the-range vehicles. In the 1930s those coaches were mainly Leylands, but WA hung back when it came to diesel engines. The company believed petrol engines gave a smoother ride and stuck with them until 1940 — late by industry standards.

Prior to World War 2 the company was based mainly in the Leeds/Bradford area and expanded by buying up other coach firms, 14 of them in the 1930s, sometimes retaining their identity — for example W. Fish, of Morley. This policy remained through much of the company's life. In 1937 Robert Barr formed a public company, the Barr & Wallace Arnold Trust, to take over his transport companies, which included both coaches and trucks. With more reliable vehicles on the market during those times, distances travelled by both types expanded considerably. Coach tours to Devon, Wales and Scotland were introduced; previously trips had mainly been concentrated on the Yorkshire Dales and the coast, the latter proving so popular that regular daily coach services were introduced, the beginnings of what was to become a major part of the business.

World War 2 brought a temporary halt to the rapid growth of the Wallace Arnold company. Vehicles were requisitioned for military use, and leisure traffic dried up. However, the company gained new work for the remaining coaches, providing services for the many businesses local to its area that were undertaking war work, particularly the Avro works at Yeadon. The scale of this work was such that second-hand purchases were made, including WA's first double-decker. In 1942 the coachbuilding firm of Wilks & Meade, based in Millwright Street, Leeds, was acquired. This was a far-sighted move intended to provide the company with skills to rebuild the fleet in the postwar years. It was to be needed.

2. POSTWAR

Following World War 2 there was a tremendous demand for leisure travel, both as a result of the lifting of wartime restrictions and as an escape from still very austere times. The industry found this demand difficult to meet, as new vehicles were in short supply. WA tackled the problem in three ways: firstly by buying as many new coaches as it could, secondly by rebuilding existing ones (this is where its own coachbuilder, Wilks & Meade, came in very useful) and thirdly by buying up other operators. This last took WA out of its traditional area, one purchase being that of Box, Castleford, which brought five new coaches.

New vehicles were largely of Leyland, AEC, Daimler and Bedford manufacture with 29- to 33-seat bodywork built in the main by Duple, Burlingham and Wilks & Meade. Petrol was no longer an economical proposition, so the company undertook a programme of converting existing heavyweight types to diesel power. Most new vehicles arrived with this type of engine, the exceptions being lightweight coaches, mainly Bedfords but also including a number of Commers, and some of these would survive until 1959.

Operations suspended for the war were restarted as soon as possible. Daily express services from Leeds to the coast — firstly Blackpool, then Bridlington, Scarborough, Filey and Southport — were very popular, and before long tours to Devon and Cornwall were back on offer. By 1949 Continental tours had been reintroduced, first to Switzerland, then France, Italy and the Netherlands. To support all this activity, booking offices were opened in many Northern towns and in London.

WA realised the value of London and the South East, not only from a British perspective but also from that of visitors from overseas, who had come to know the capital in particular during the war years, so in 1948 it acquired Homeland Tours, of Croydon. This company, set up by one Francis Flin Senior, had run high-quality tours before the war. As with so many things with which WA became involved the deal came about as a result of Robert Barr's identifying its potential, following

a chance meeting with Francis. Initially tours started from Park Lane in Croydon, the departure point later moving to Fairfield Halls. The conditions of this arrangement stipulated that coaches had to be away by 9.30am, which explains why few people were aware of WA's significant presence in the area.

By 1948 the Government of the day was talking about nationalisation. In that year's Annual Report Robert Barr was dismissive of this in respect of coach operators such as WA, and, although he sold his lorry business to British Road Services (in 1949), WA was quick to re-establish itself and looking to expand.

Above: A photograph re-enacted over many decades with different coaches and different groups of happy holidaymakers. A Burlingham-bodied Leyland Tiger poses behind a group in the late 1940s who were probably not as old as they appear at first glance. Either they all used the same optician or they were on a trip to a Arthur Askey lookalike convention.
Stephen Barber collection

Left: New in 1949 and seen here with its original Wilks & Meade body, doing what it was built to do, Daimler CVD6 MUM 460 was destined to become a Roe-bodied double-decker in 1956, thereafter serving Farsley Omnibus until transferred to Kippax Motors in 1967. (Sister vehicle MUM 461 is shown in rebuilt form on page 56.) WA clearly paid its 'subs', as there's an AA badge on the radiator. *Stephen Barber collection*

Below left: One of the earliest Plaxton bodies in the fleet was carried by EYG 582, one of four similar AEC Regals purchased in 1946 with the fleet of M. Box of Castleford, shortly after it was delivered. Sold in 1955, it went on to work for Wimpey (contractor). Roy Marshall / *Stephen Barber collection*

Above: The 1949 carefree holiday brochure included Scotland, Devon, the South Coast, Paris, Cannes, Nice, the Italian Riviera and Switzerland.

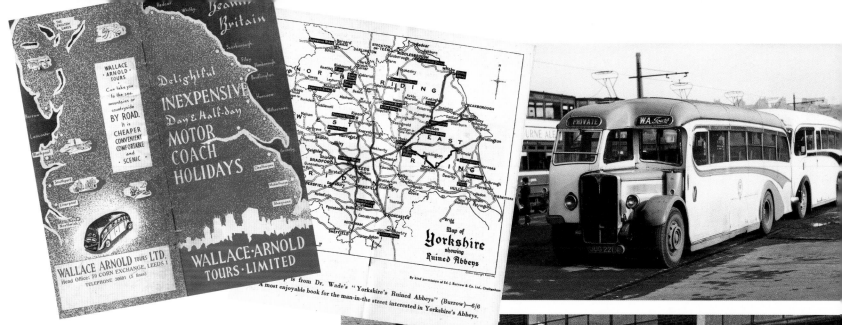

Above: Late-1940s motor-coach holidays, with a charming map featuring Yorkshire's ruined abbeys. Places visited are described in full detail, in line with Robert Barr's vision, and from this we learn that both Ripley Castle and a cottage in Tockwith claim Oliver Cromwell spent the night there after the Battle of Marston Moor in 1644. (Tockwith was perhaps the better bet, for at Ripley he was given a cool reception, being placed under the personal surveillance of Dame Ingilby, who wore in her girdle a couple of loaded pistols.)

Above right: Not as it first appears, AEC Regal JUG 221 was originally licensed in 1933 as VY 4477 by a company in York. At the start of World War 2, it was requisitioned by the Ministry of Transport for use by the Royal Air Force. Purchased by WA from the MoS in 1943, it was re-registered in 1946 and re-engined with a diesel unit. In 1948 it received this new Burlingham body. Quite a tale. It is seen here in a classic Leeds line-up of trams and coaches on Lowfields Road, having brought Leeds United supporters to the nearby Elland Road football ground. *R. F. Mack / Stephen Barber collection*

Right: Although of limited capacity (29 seats), the Bedford OB was reliable and more importantly available in the early postwar years. This 1949 example, MUA 346, has the usual Duple body, but with an unusual side moulding scheme. It was transferred to bus routes at Hardwicks in 1954 and sold in 1955.
Stephen Barber collection

Tour brochure from 1951, featuring the coach that went to the New York World Automotive Fair and including details of the company's latest underfloor-engined types.

In many ways the 1950s and '60s were the golden age of coaching, WA's experience being no exception. Many of the features of those times lasted into the 1970s and '80s and will take up a lot of our time on this journey. Coach travel, despite the postwar rise of the private car, remained hugely popular — in 1959, for example, the express-service operation alone carried more than 80,000 passengers — and the company prided itself on predicting future trends. Let us look at some of the highlights on this part of our tour.

Things didn't start out too well. By 1950 mainstream vehicle manufacturers were beginning to produce underfloor-engined single-deck chassis. These not only permitted an increase in seating capacity — typically from around 33 to 41 — but also allowed a full front to be fitted, giving a sleek, modern appearance (although some bodybuilders were more successful at this than others). What it most certainly did was to make WA's new fleet of postwar half-cab coaches and Bedford OBs look dated overnight. WA responded to this by embarking upon an extensive programme of rebuilding, rebodying and body-swapping involving 116 coaches in its existing fleet whilst standardising on the underfloor-engined types when it came to new deliveries.

The new types were fitted with a centre entrance, an arrangement WA would continue to favour until 1966 (1967 in Devon) — late by industry standards. The theory was that passengers mixed better when moving from both ends of the vehicle and got to know each other by using the centre door — something that did not happen when queuing to alight at the front.

In 1950 the red trim was dropped from the livery, leaving coaches in plain ivory — a style that was to remain throughout most of the company's existence.

Property was not neglected, and notable was the opening, in 1957, of a coach station in Leeds city centre at The Calls, dramatically reducing congestion in the area. In 1966 the Leeds fleet moved to a brand-new facility in Gelderd Road, vacating the long-established depot in Hunslet Road. The new site boasted departure bays, maintenance facilities and offices.

Coach tours were the cornerstone of the company, and wherever possible a WA vehicle was provided. For non-tour operations huge numbers of coaches were hired in from local operators, many of which depended on WA for much of their work. But coach tours were very seasonal, and to gain extra revenue WA introduced Elderly Persons' tours — or 'Dream Holidays for the Elderly', as they were originally called — aimed at the over-65s; indeed, at first a pension book had to be produced when making a booking. The age limit was later reduced to 55. Although it seems likely that the idea was pioneered c1953 by Cyril Littlewood of Sheffield, WA made it a major part of the business, providing lucrative work in September and October, and again in April and May. However, mainstream hotels would not cut their prices, so WA started to use cheap accommodation that amounted to little more than glorified guest houses.

As ever, WA sought to maximise its revenue and in the late 1960s was charging £29 for a week when the hotel cost only £11 — although WA, like many at the time, preferred to use the more upmarket-sounding 'guinea' (£1.05). Expectations tended to be higher than the product could justify, resulting in frequent complaints, and Geoffrey Steel, then Programme Manager, recalls dealing with a wide variety. Some people were not content merely to complain about their breakfast bacon — they actually sent examples through the post. One establishment in Dunoon felt peanut salad was a suitable main course for dinner, whilst when investigating a report of cold chips in Torquay Geoffrey discovered that the owner had never cooked before and that his cooking fat was not hot enough. Complaints of tinned meat being used exclusively in a seaside establishment resulted in a visit by Geoffrey. The interview, conducted in the basement living quarters of the owner, who hailed from Birmingham, resulted in a complete denial of all charges along with the offer: "Oi'll show yer me butcher's bills, Mr Steel!".

Complaints aside, the Elderly Persons' tours were, in the main, a Godsend, although there was one drawback — they overlapped with the principal tours at the beginning and end of the main season, and covering all commitments sometimes required the provision of up to 120 coaches over and above the scheduled 100 tour coaches. Stephen Barber recalls that the two sections never spoke to each other about vehicle requirements and that for a few weeks it would be an operational nightmare.

If WA skimped somewhat on its Elderly Persons' tours, the same could not be said of its main-season tours, which were splendid affairs of high quality. Organising these was the responsibility of Robert Barr's eldest daughter, Margaret Hook, and her approach was one of being very cost-conscious whilst taking no risks. Members of WA management recall her visits (she lived in Edinburgh) as 'interfering and wreaking

havoc'. The same people, however, are unanimous in their opinion that she knew exactly how to put together a good tour and was one of the industry's most knowledgeable operators. Indeed, she became the first female President of the Association of British Travel Agents, no mean achievement. Barbara Flin, niece of Robert Barr, describes her as 'a brilliant businesswoman'.

Major Elphee was a tour driver based in Bradford in the late 1950s before moving to Devon. He recalls his first tour to Paignton. He was given an aged Bedford, 'despite there being three new coaches in the depot'. In Bristol the Bedford broke down, and a call to Leeds elicited the information that he would have to sort it out himself. He managed to hire a coach locally, so, having missed tea in Cheddar, he arranged dinner in a local hotel, at the end of which the head waiter presented him with a bill for £18, then a considerable sum. Successfully redirecting that to Leeds, he arrived in Paignton at 1am.

The following morning Margaret Hook appeared in the hotel demanding an explanation, saying that, had she been there, she would have done things differently. Major pointed out that she hadn't been there. She then asked where the coach was, to which Major replied that it would be ready

Above: No colour pictures have been located of the original 'red and ivory' livery, but this view using a computer program giving the present day effect of colour tinting of 1947 Duple-bodied AEC Regal KUM 386 gives an idea. In 1952 it was transferred to upgrade the newly acquired Hardwicks fleet and therefore missed the turmoil of rebuilding and rebodying that took place. It was withdrawn, untouched, in 1955, and, amazingly, its chassis survives in Malta, where a group of dedicated preservations led by Peter Skerry hope to construct a replacement for the original body. *Stephen Barber collection, digital representation by Garry Luck*

Right: A Leyland PS1 new in 1947 with a Burlingham body, KUM 362 was involved only marginally in the extensive programme of upgrading and rebuilding upon which WA embarked in the early 1950s. In 1953 it received the 1950 Duple body shown here from a 1949 Leyland PS2, which later in the year received its *third* body following lengthening of its chassis to 30ft. KUM 362 made do with just two and was withdrawn in 1958. Its original body ended up on a 1938 Leyland TS8.
Stephen Barber collection

Left: Most of the new bodies fitted during the rebuilding process came from Plaxton. However, in 1952 these two 1949 AEC Regals lost their Burlingham bodies and received these unusual (and rather unattractive) Bellhouse-Hartwell bodies. Both spent their final months with Farsley Omnibus before withdrawal in 1958.
Stephen Barber collection

Below: 'Dream holidays for the Elderly' from Devon in 1965, showing what you could get for your guinea.

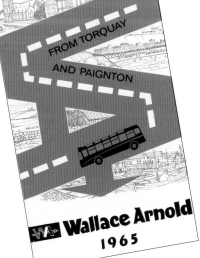

DREAM HOLIDAYS FOR THE ELDERLY

MINIMUM AGE 50

FROM TORQUAY AND PAIGNTON

VA Wallace Arnold

1965

Above and left: These two vehicles show the rebodying policy taken to its extremes. Both Leyland PS2s, they were new in 1950 with attractive full-front Burlingham bodies but received new Plaxton bodywork in time for the 1953 season, their original bodies being mounted on older chassis. One year later the new Plaxton bodies were removed and passed on. Both chassis were lengthened, and yet another new Plaxton body (this time 30ft long) fitted as seen here. NUA 751 is seen at Redcar Races, where it appears to be the object of much flat-cap speculation. Alongside is an unusual Strachans-bodied AEC Reliance of Scott's Grey's, Darlington, which seems to be attracting admiring glances. In the second picture NUA 752 poses for the official Plaxton photographer on Marine Drive, Scarborough, before the signwriting was applied to the boot. Both PS2s were sold in 1959.
Stephen Barber collection (both)

Wallace Arnold 72

Dream Holidays for the Older Holidaymaker

SPECIALLY REDUCED PRICES

British and Continental Holidays from Yorkshire

Wallace Arnold
nice people to go with

Dream Holidays in Britain '74

The friendly way around beautiful Britain–at specially reduced prices for older holidaymakers. **from London**

in Bristol, whereupon Margaret immediately delegated her husband, William (who was also High Sheriff in Edinburgh and was known at WA as Sheriff Hook) to take Major to Bristol in their car. The children came too, and on the way they visited Glastonbury and took lunch at Wells Cathedral, William explaining he wanted the children to see these places. Clearly it was a family holiday, and Major remembers William as a 'lovely chap'.

Tours were planned in meticulous detail, and the following extract from an early (1949) brochure provides a taster of what was on offer. The Western Highlands & Oban 'B' tour, running on 18 occasions between May and September, took in Edinburgh, Oban, Loch Lomond, Loch Katrine, the Trossachs, Peebles and the English Lake District over seven days for £15 15s 0d (£15.75). Each day's journey was detailed, as were the hotels for each night, complete with phone numbers, *e.g.*: 'the Royal Hotel at Oban, phone Oban 2802'. The description tells of 'heather-clad hills, the bluebells of Scotland and the sweet country air, with its tang of pine and bracken', prospective passengers being assured that they will be 'held spellbound by the glories of sparkling lochs and colourful tartans' and that they will return home 'through the glorious Lake District, feeling regret at leaving this land of poetic beauty'. It has, of course, to finish with a poem:

Ah there my young footsteps in infancy wandered
My cap was the bonnet, my cloak was the plaid,
On chieftains long perished my memory pondered,
As gaily I strode through the pine-covered glade.

What more can you say?

The hotel industry certainly recognised the role that WA played in its business. A journalist from the *Yorkshire Evening Post* recalls spending the night with his wife in a hotel in Hull and pleading poverty. His plea elicited a very favourable rate for dinner, bed and breakfast, and on examining his receipt he found that it read: 'Special terms — two Wallace Arnold coach drivers'.

Following Robert Barr's death in 1961 his son, Malcolm, took over as Chairman. One of Robert's last actions was to

see off a record-breaking tour to Moscow, and, although this was not repeated for many years, WA could by this time claim to offer holidays from Orkney to Ibiza, using coaches, trains and aeroplanes.

Left: What a magnificent vehicle. OUA 814 was one of 13 Burlingham Seagulls (10 Leyland Royal Tigers and three AEC Regal IVs) that arrived in 1951. Overnight the half-cabs and Bedford OBs in their red and ivory colours looked old-fashioned; no wonder the company decided upon such a dramatic rebuilding programme. The Seagull was the most successful body design for underfloor-engined coaches, and on Leyland Royal Tiger and Tiger Cub chassis and the equivalent AEC Regal IV and Reliance it became the archetypical WA coach of the 1950s. OUA 814 was withdrawn at the end of the 1960 season but with three others was kept for the carriage of Royal Mail parcels over the Christmas period. *Stephen Barber collection*

Right: WA was not the only concern attracted by the Burlingham Seagull. The then still-independent Feather Bros, before purchase by WA in 1955, acquired four AEC Regal IVs so bodied. In this splendid view GKY 960 — a 1951 example — is on tour in London, being seen against a familiar background. Could that be Churchill's fine car emerging from the House of Commons on a matter of high state, or is it just someone going for lunch?
Arthur Hustwit Memorial Collection @ NA3T

16

Left and below left: Alongside the new underfloor-engined types, a few lightweights entered the fleet. Although much cheaper, they could carry only 33 passengers compared with the 41 of the new heavyweights. OUM 854 was a 1951 Duple-bodied Bedford SB, PNW 303 a 1952 Plaxton-bodied Commer Avenger. For all its apparent size, OUM 854 could carry only four more passengers than the traditional Bedford OB.
Stephen Barber collection (both)

Right: Duple's answer to the Burlingham Seagull, the Ambassador, was not quite as stylish but nevertheless made up most of the WA 1952 order, bodying all the Royal Tigers and three Regal IVs. The other three AECs were bodied by that up and coming Scarborough company — Plaxton. Normal service resumed in 1953 when more Seagulls arrived in Leeds. *Vic Nutten / Stephen Barber collection*

Right: These Plaxton Venturer-bodied AEC Reliances were new in 1954 and came with the Kitchin's business. The view shows the rear end of NWW 803. At this time Plaxton offered the option of the rear centre screens being turned outwards which changed the vehicle's appearance considerably. These coaches are shown at the premises of coach dealer Stanley Hughes in 1967, following withdrawal. They had been transferred to the main WA fleet and repainted in ivory in 1966. No 803 shows the places credited as home towns. *Stephen Barber collection*

18

Left: UUB 931 was a lone Sentinel SLC6 purchased by WA to support the sister motor dealership which at that time had a Sentinel franchise. Exhibiting it at the 1954 Commercial Motor Show and entering it in the first British Coach Rally, at Clacton, WA did its best to market the vehicle, but sales of the type were limited. UUB 931 had a Burlingham Seagull body with the additional side moulding and a chrome company emblem. It is seen here taking part at Clacton in the company of a Weymann Fanfare-bodied AEC Reliance owned by Robin Hood of Nottingham, later to be taken over by Barton Transport. *Roy Marshall / Stephen Barber collection*

Right: Four Duple-bodied coaches entered service in 1954, none in 1955 and two in 1956. All were AEC Reliances, and one of the 1954 coaches — SUG 5, with Ambassador Coronation bodywork — is shown resting while on tour. *Kevin Lane / Stephen Barber collection*

Left: One of the pair of Reliance/Duples delivered in 1956, Elizabethan-bodied WUM 44 is shown here in Blackpool in 1957 dwarfed by one of the local inhabitants, which may have been Perry Cliff's first sighting. *R. B. Parr / Stephen Barber collection*

Left: The best customer for Sentinel Coaches during WA's dealership of the type was Schofield's of Marsden, which purchased four with Burlingham coachwork. LWR 985, a 1952 Duple Ambassador-bodied Leyland Royal Tiger, was taken in part exchange and fitted in well with WA's similar vehicles. The driver in the fine white coat, preventing the vehicle from leaving the road, was Les 'Cannonball' Selby, who became (in)famous for his role in a 1960s television documentary about the life of a coach driver. Revelations about alleged drivers' 'fiddles' and nocturnal habits did nothing to endear him to colleagues. *D. Akrigg / Stephen Barber collection*

Right: 1956 saw the arrival of the first front-entrance Burlingham Seagulls comprising 10 Leyland Tiger Cubs and one AEC Reliance. Here XNW 52, on a tour from London to the Isle of Skye, awaits its passengers who have spent the night in the Griffin Hotel in Leeds. Parked in Boar Lane alongside the tram tracks, it is outside a shop, the political correctness of which would be questioned today.
M. A. Taylor / Stephen Barber collection

Right: 'Nothing new under the sun' is a common statement in the PSV industry. Here the solitary Leyland Tiger Cub of 1956, YUG 100, carrying trade plate 563 TB, shows the Continental exit arrangement of its Plaxton Consort body. It was part of the order for 1957 — a quiet year for new coaches (only eight purchased), reflecting the effect of the Suez Crisis — and is seen at that year's Commercial Motor Show alongside Daimler CVG6/Willowbrook VKV 99, one of the earliest double-deck buses built to the newly legalised 30ft maximum length.
Stephen Barber collection

Left: 1958 was a bumper year for new coaches and for Plaxton. Owing to a strike Duple was unable fulfil its bodywork order for a batch of 20 AEC Reliances, and thus began WA's long relationship with Plaxton. Here newly delivered 8327 U, with Consort II coachwork, stands outside the depot on Hunslet Road. Another of this batch, 8332 U, survives today in preservation (see page 1). *John Cockshott / Stephen Barber collection*

Right: If 1958 saw the start of Plaxton dominance it also saw the end of Burlingham as a WA supplier. A batch of six very attractive Tiger Cubs, among them 8339 U, seen here in London, marked the end of the Seagull era. *John Cockshott / Stephen Barber collection*

Right: 1959 saw the development of Plaxton body styles with the introduction of its dramatic Panorama. WA took a batch of seven but also kept a foot in the traditional camp with vehicles such as Consort IV-bodied 9200 NW, seen here. WA's preference for centre entrances meant that slightly dated, sliding-window-type bodies would join the fleet for many years, but this multi-windowed AEC Reliance has a certain charm.
A. J. Douglas / Stephen Barber collection

Left: Duple's reworked Britannia style obviously caught WA's eye, six joining the fleet in 1959. Three of them, including 4327 UA shown here at The Calls in Leeds, were hired from a dealer and spent only one year in the fleet. Note the company's various products displayed on the hand-painted board behind the coach.
John Cockshott / Stephen Barber collection

23

Right: 1960 brought another large batch of AEC Reliance/ Plaxtons. Here Embassy-bodied 5639 UB prepares to leave Harrogate bus station, having dropped off passengers from an Isle of Skye tour. They obviously dressed expecting the worst. Also joining the fleet in 1960 was a large batch of Fords, about to enjoy success in the WA fleet as a supplier of lightweights. More important, however, was the arrival of the first Leyland Leopard, which type was to become the company's first choice for chassis until the end of the 1970s. *Stephen Barber collection*

Left: Most of the Fords supplied in the 1960s had Duple bodies, but this 1960 example had Plaxton Consort IV bodywork. Here 5648 UB awaits its Morecambe-bound passengers in Morley Street, Bradford, when almost new. No doubt some will remember certain of the performers appearing at the famous Bradford Alhambra. *John Cockshott / Stephen Barber collection*

Left: Morley Street, Bradford, the centre of operations in that city. Here 1961 AEC Reliance 9926 UG, with Plaxton Embassy body, has returned from a tour to Torquay, and passengers clutching their cases are crossing the road to catch a service bus home — hope they've spotted that Ford Zephyr. Behind is a similar but year-older Reliance in Feather Bros livery.
Stephen Barber collection

Right: A rare rear view of 1961 Leyland Leopard/Plaxton Embassy 9903 UG parked at the new Gelderd Road depot. This colour shot shows the interior trim, with grey moquette on the seat backs.
Stephen Barber collection

Few now remember that, prior to 1980, all coach operations had to be licensed by the Traffic Commissioners. Achieving this was Geoffrey Steel's role when Licensing Officer, with two members of staff and 27 filing cabinets. Whilst it was a year-round task, the winter months were the most active, when the operations side of the business was quieter. Main licences would be obtained to reach destinations, and applications made for trips out from that destination; these were known as fantails. Full details of individual starting points and of all roads travelled had to be shown, and just keeping things up-to-date was a major task. Matters were not made any easier by the fact that, since the system was

established in 1930, strange restrictions had grown up from town to town. In some cases WA did not have its own licences, instead running 'on hire' to a local operator, paying to use its licence. A good example of this was the European tour programme, WA having no licences to operate between London and the South Coast ferry ports and running 'on hire' to the likes of Royal Blue and East Kent.

Obtaining licences was a contentious business, local operators frequently being vociferous in their objections. This meant that Traffic Commissioners' hearings often took many days, and Malcolm Barr's legal background came in very useful. Objections came from various sources.

Right: One-off vehicles often attract most attention, as was the case with 649 CNW, a solitary Harrington Cavalier-bodied AEC Reliance hired from a dealer for the 1962 season. Its location at Victoria Coach Station is interesting; it is working a trip from Yorkshire to Cliftonville, and for good utilisation has been used to transport Europe-bound holidaymakers from London to the Channel coast. WA had no licence for this, and would be working 'on hire' to East Kent. Note the additional step in the form of a beer crate — a far cry from today's access legislation. *D. F. Parker / Stephen Barber collection*

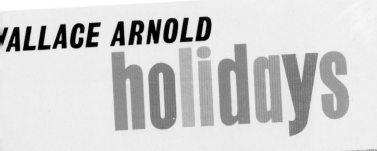

WALLACE ARNOLD
holidays

programme from Yorkshire **Britain & Ireland 1965**

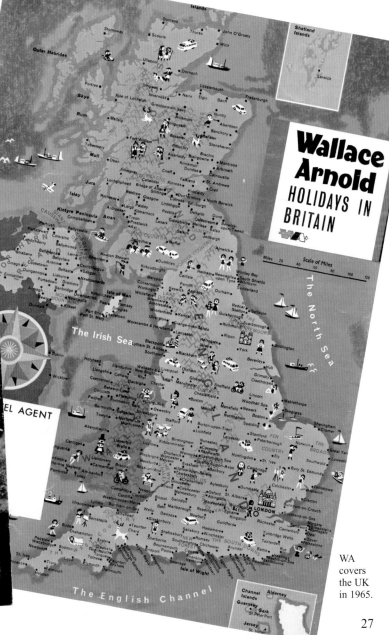

Wallace Arnold
HOLIDAYS IN BRITAIN

WA covers the UK in 1965.

27

Applications for additional pick-up points for tours originating from the capital elicited an objection from London Transport, which maintained that customers could reach their holiday coach by catching a bus. Pick-ups in Leicester received an objection from Midland Red — withdrawn only when local travel agents threatened to stop selling Midland Red products. Of course, London itself was a major draw, attracting a vast array of operators both locally and from outside the capital. Grey-Green provided only mini-breaks from suburbia, whilst Royal Blue offered holidays using its express services and adding in a hotel.

Evan Evans sightseeing brochure from 1974.

With a large presence in the capital, WA was part of an unofficial grouping of four companies known collectively as the 'String Quartet' — the other three being Galleon Tours, Glenton Tours and Southdown. The idea was to keep others out of the lucrative London market, rather than there being any common ground. It was a marriage of convenience, as in reality they pretty much loathed each other. Southdown, for example, didn't regard WA as a serious competitor, while, conversely, former WA Managing Director John King recalls Southdown as 'too snobbish'. In 1969 WA attempted to break into the overseas market by purchasing the long-established London coach firm of Evan Evans. This was a very different beast, its workings being heavily entwined with the unique London market, and it never fulfilled WA's hopes for it. Indeed, in many ways it proved a burden.

But Scotland was to provide the largest battles. Although coach holidays were a sideline to its bus operation, the Scottish Bus Group (SBG) simply did not want anyone else on its patch, particularly anyone from south of the border. WA was anxious to become established, as the Barrs were of Scottish descent and, besides having a feel for the country, could see the profit potential. WA had additionally bought a hotel in Grantown-on-Spey.

Although the company wanted to sell tours within Scotland it realised that it was unlikely ever to be given the opportunity and so decided to sell England and Wales to the Scots. Applications were vigorously opposed by SBG, so in 1963 WA finally got around the problem by buying a Scottish company, Dickson's of Dundee. Dickson's main office, at 45 Reform Street, sported a splendid tiled floor showing a steam locomotive (an LMS streamlined 'Coronation' Pacific), a plane, a ship and a car. Geoffrey Steel recalls a modern fleet, his abiding memory being, in the winter of 1963/4, of helping to drive the coaches down to Leeds for repainting in WA livery — a key part of the plan to let the SBG know that there was a 'new kid on the block'.

Dickson's also had strategic offices at 354 Sauchiehall Street, Glasgow, and one in Edinburgh, so the scene was set for a showdown. WA produced a 'spoof' tours brochure, and staff including John King and Geoffrey Steel went around Glasgow and Edinburgh, knocking on doors to drum up support. They both remember the different receptions. In Glasgow, although approaching tenement buildings may have been a touch nerve-racking, once inside they usually received a warm welcome. Geoffrey recalls: 'You were sat down in a snug front room in front of a blazing fire and given a cup of tea.' In Edinburgh, by contrast, there was a single-bar electric fire — and no tea. Nevertheless, the plan worked, and, come the day of the Traffic Commissioner's hearing into WA's tour applications, a band of 50 supporters packed the courtroom. Cross-examining one of the witnesses, who claimed she wanted to go to Scarborough, the SBG lawyer retorted that his client offered trips to Bridlington, which was just the same. This provoked uproar from the gallery, and the furious commissioner cleared the court. Someone whispered to Geoffrey: "That's what you get if you mix Rangers and Celtic supporters!"

Finally WA got its licences and, by linking them with other licences, grew the Scottish market considerably. Bournemouth and the Isle of Wight, for example, often saw up to seven tours a week, and Geoffrey recalls coaches 'going up and down all the time'.

Less stressful was the purchase of a company and the consequent takeover of its licences. In this way WA spread throughout most of the country, although the North West of England was denied it, there being a number of very strong local operators. Geoffrey Steel felt that WA became obsessed with operators with Excursion & Tour licences. A huge coup was the acquisition in the early 1960s of such licences held by state-owned United Counties, based in Northampton. Apparently other state-owned companies were livid, but again, as with so many things, the takeover had come about as a result of a friendship that Robert Barr had made. It was a good move: in terms of passenger numbers Northampton was always in WA's top 10.

Excursions provided a huge source of revenue, in particular from the company's home patch of Leeds and Bradford. An extensive programme was offered in a very competitive market where, prior to the Transport Act 1980, WA faced many licensed operators. In Leeds were West Yorkshire, Samuel Ledgard, Heaps Tours and Rogers (later part of Heaps), while West Yorkshire and Ledgard were also in Bradford. Key acquisitions of Kitchin's of Pudsey and Wardways of Bingley had consolidated WA's licences, but much time was spent by the Licensing Department in adding new destinations, many made possible by the expanding motorway network. Much of this work involved fighting off the efforts of competitors to do likewise, but, interestingly, the rules prior to 1980 required all operators to charge the same fare. Today's competition authorities would have had a field-day.

Every excursion was linked, picking up in Leeds, Pudsey and Bradford if travelling west, or starting in Bradford if heading east. This ensured a paying load even on quiet days, but pick-ups would soon normally be split, one coach serving Bradford and Pudsey, another Leeds. To the most popular destinations, such as Blackpool, Scarborough and Bridlington, duplicates were commonplace and on summer Sundays would usually run into double figures. Holiday weeks and bank holidays saw huge numbers of coaches required to meet demand. Stephen Barber recalls that one of his early tasks was to help excursion staff on busy departures, particularly on Easter Monday 1970, when more than 50 coaches departed from Leeds and a similar number from Bradford. Smaller excursion programmes were run from the Castleford area, and also from Scarborough to cater for holidaymakers in the resort. Wallace Arnold (Devon), to which we shall return later, operated an extensive programme of sightseeing excursions for holidaymakers in Torquay and Paignton in competition with Grey Cars, the coaching arm of Devon General, a British Electric Traction company. Although competitive, it was a gentlemanly arrangement, with a cosy agreement on fares.

In hindsight it may seem strange that WA brought so many licensing battles upon itself, but the WA team point out that everything the company did was competitive; it had no market to itself. The battles for licences were defensive first and foremost, but, as Geoffrey Steel recalls, 'Sometimes, to defend you have to attack'.

The licensing system provided protection for established operators, even if, on occasion, it did not exactly operate in the public interest. However, it did go a long way towards controlling the activities of illegal or fly-by-night firms. But to established excursion operators, other firms, legal or illegal, were not the biggest threat; this was the private party — the notice displayed in a shop window or on a notice board: 'Social club coach excursion to Scarborough, 7.30 Saturday, ring 12345'. Over this there was no control. Churches, exempt under Schedule 12 of the Transport Act 1930, were often the worst offenders.

Left: The increase in permitted length to 36ft for the 1962 season did not benefit the fleet appearance-wise. A stretched version of the 1961 Plaxton Embassy body as shown here on 76 BUA came a poor second to Plaxton's sleek Panorama style of the same year. By 1962 the Leyland Leopard had taken over from the AEC Reliance as the preferred heavyweight chassis, 13 being delivered, compared with just seven Reliances.
M. King / Stephen Barber collection

Right: A later example of retaining identities. The first examples of the Plaxton Panorama, albeit with modifications to meet WA requirements, arrived in 1963. Here AEC Reliance 117 EUA, allocated to Feather Bros but now in Kitchin livery, shows the non-standard centre door and sliding windows that were to remain part of the WA specification until 1966.
Stephen Barber collection

Left: A typical WA coach of the mid-1960s. The 1964 deliveries were identical to those of the previous year, as demonstrated here by Leyland Leopard 201 HUM. Although the bodywork was a modified version of the Panorama, the coaches were badged as Embassys.
M. King / Stephen Barber collection

Right: While Gelderd Road was being built the coaches were based at Donisthorpe Street, formerly a Leeds City Transport depot, their former home on Hunslet Road being redeveloped as a car and truck dealership. This April 1964 view features newly delivered 208 HUM standing among the dereliction with some older members of the fleet.
John Cockshott / Stephen Barber collection

Left: This rear view of a 1964 Plaxton Panorama-bodied Bedford VAL14 shows the reference on the boot to the Dickson business taken over the previous year. The policy was to impose the Wallace Arnold name as quickly as possible. WA was a big user of the Bedford VAL but had to work hard to overcome the inherent braking problems resulting from the wheel arrangement. This view is taken on the forecourt of the Stanley Hughes premises alongside the A58. Today it is little changed in the ownership of Arriva Bus & Coach.
John Cockshott / Stephen Barber collection

Left: A quiet time on Morley Street Bradford, awaiting the arrival of passengers. A 1965 Feather Bros VAL14/Plaxton Panorama is parked ahead of two 1959 WA AEC Reliances. Wonderful. *Colin Temple / Stuart Jones collection*

Right: One of the legacies of the Evan Evans purchase was Plaxton Panorama I-bodied Ford R226 KPM 386E, built to sightseeing specification for use in London. It spent its final year working from Scarborough depot, where the sightseeing locations were very different indeed. *Andrew Wiltshire collection*

Above: 1967 saw the standardisation on front-entrance Plaxton Panorama I-bodied Leyland Leopards. JUA 314E was a 10-metre PSU4 model for tours to Rothesay and Dunoon, where ferry sizes imposed length restrictions. Originally in Feathers red and grey, it was repainted into the new grey fleet livery in 1970.
Stephen Barber collection

Right: 1969 heralded the new grey livery along with a large batch of 35 new Plaxton Panorama Elites mounted on the now standard Leopard chassis. RUB 356G was sent to fly the flag at both the Blackpool and Brighton coach rallies. It is seen here at the former displaying a full set of travelling rugs — coach heaters were not too efficient in those days.
Stephen Barber collection

Left: One of the exhibits on the Plaxton stand at the 1968 Commercial Motor Show was RUA 713G, Wallace Arnold's last Bedford VAL, a Panorama Elite-bodied VAL70 (three went to Evan Evans in 1969). This picture gives a good impression of how the combination of their length and small wheels made these coaches look even longer. The livery was subsequently amended slightly with the removal of the dark grey window surrounds to lighten the appearance. This coach demonstrates an early example of tinted windows.
Stephen Barber collection

Right: 1971 was noteworthy for late delivery of Leyland chassis. Some were cancelled and replaced with AEC and Ford vehicles hired from Stanley Hughes. This line-up at Gelderd Road includes three of the resulting 1971 AEC Reliance/ Plaxton Panorama Elite IIs. *Stephen Barber collection*

Right: A German in Yorkshire. Also new in 1971 was this Mercedes-Benz O.302. Mercedes-Benz was making a play for the British market and targeted key fleets like WA and Grey-Green with demonstrators. It also offered to supply WA with vehicles at the same price as Plaxton-bodied Leopards, a tempting offer indeed. But it was rejected and DLC 950J remained unique in the WA fleet until the arrival 20 years later of five Plaxton-bodied Mercedes-Benz O.303s. *Stephen Barber collection*

Above and right: When they did finally arrive this is what the Plaxton Panorama Elite II-bodied Leyland Leopards of 1971 looked like. These official shots were taken by WA and show the full effect of the new livery and the interior, still requiring travel rugs when the temperature dropped.
Stephen Barber collection (both)

Wallace Arnold
Great British Holidays 1972
Scenic Touring · Leisure centred · Pleasure packed
Programme from SCOTLAND

Magnificent scenery

It's all mapped out for you

Steeped in History

Good Food

Holiday Cavalcade

Ride in style

Coastal Beauty

Rural Charm

Peace and tranquility

Hand picked Hotels

Left: An Evan Evans publicity shot taken in 1971 shows smart drivers and a variety of Plaxton Panorama Elite-bodied Leopards and Bedford VALs and VAMs. The WA coach (second left), brought in to add volume, is one of the 10m 1970 Leopards intended for use on Rothesay & Dunoon tours. *Stephen Barber collection*

Right: Towards the end of their lives many coaches ended up on the RCA Fylingdales contract in North Yorkshire. A product of the Cold War, the early warning station on the moors above Whitby was security conscious and provided its own drivers for staff transport. WA serviced the coaches and provided spare vehicles in the event of a breakdown, of which there were sadly plenty. Here AUA 420J, an Elite II-bodied Leopard, is seen parked between duties in the livery variation used for this contract. *Stuart Jones*

Although known primarily as an extended-tour operator, right up until the 1980s WA was also the leading general coaching concern in the West Riding's two major cities of Leeds and Bradford. As such it provided an extensive private-hire service, booking everything from local school visits to extended private tours, both in the UK and on the Continent, although on summer Saturdays such bookings were strictly controlled, every available vehicle, owned or hired, being required for the company's express services.

Depots at Royston and Castleford served mining areas, where there was a strong tradition of working men's clubs, all of which organised an annual Sunday outing to the seaside. Around 20 coaches would be required, so it was essential to ensure that no more than two such jobs were booked on any one day, bearing in mind that the two depots could provide only about 35 coaches between them. Leeds occasionally took on such jobs, and Stephen Barber remembers, early on in his WA career, in 1969, supervising the departure of 35 coaches bound for Blackpool on hire to the Middleton Tenants' Association. All coaches were numbered, the sole WA vehicle being, obviously, No 1, and were lined up in order around the Gelderd Road site before setting off in convoy to Middleton — what a sight that must have been.

Mrs E. Martin of Halton recalls her father, a friend of Robert Barr, was president of the East End Park Working Men's Club in Leeds and ran the club's holiday fund, into which members paid a few pence each week throughout the year from August until the following August — the month the club organised its annual trip to Blackpool by WA coach.

EXECUTIVE COACHES FOR GROUP CHARTER

Wallace Arnold

A special fleet available for hire for group travel

Left: A break from the Leopard/Plaxton combination occurred in 1972 with the arrival of a batch of Duple Viceroy-bodied Leylands. Here EUG 474K stands in Edinburgh during July 1974. One cannot help thinking the painter has got the two shades of grey transposed, leaving the logo looking a bit isolated.
Kevin Lane / Stephen Barber collection

WA's express licences, which had been an important part of the company's activities since the early 1930s, were mainly summer coastal express services from its Yorkshire heartland. Competition, in particular from state-owned West Yorkshire Road Car of Harrogate and its partners (oddly mostly BET companies) and British Railways, which still regarded anything remotely long-distance as its by right, hampered development. Attempts to obtain a licence to Llandudno were always fiercely opposed by the operators of the Newcastle–Manchester/Liverpool service. Similar attempts, dating back to the 1950s, to establish a substantive service to the West Country were only finally resolved in 1968 with the creation of the 'South West Clipper' pool, which, amazingly, brought all the previous combatants together. WA became an active participant, always volunteering for the longest runs. By now you'll not be surprised to learn that these, whilst operationally taxing, were the most profitable.

Summer Saturday express services were operated to the most popular East and West Coast resorts as well as to more far-flung destinations such as Skegness and Great Yarmouth. Licensing restrictions resulted in various periods of operation, pick-ups in some towns being restricted to their annual Wakes (holiday) weeks. The key to successful — and therefore profitable — express operation was to ensure that there was no empty (or 'dead') running. On the shorter routes coaches went out in the morning, returning in the afternoon. On longer runs, to such as Great Yarmouth and Torquay, coaches departed on Friday evening, travelling overnight and returning from the resort on Saturday morning. Convenient though it may have been to travel overnight on Friday, passengers probably required a fair bit of their holiday to get over it.

A booking system was put in place to give customer confidence that he or she was guaranteed a place. In practice, bookings were taken up to the last minute — which, of course, put pressure on the Operations Department and required a high degree of crystal-ball-gazing when it came to decide how many coaches should be provided for any given departure. To simplify matters, seat numbers were not issued, the system being based on total numbers. No one with a valid ticket was ever refused travel, even if the agent through which they had booked had 'forgotten' to advise the express-service chart room.

One of the most complicated services was that serving the popular resorts of Scarborough, Filey and Bridlington and known to staff as the 'SFB'. On an average summer Saturday this service would carry between 800 and 1,000 passengers in each direction from around 16 pick-up points to five drop-off points; the journey permutations were almost endless. Normally all coaches would be hired from local operators, a WA driver travelling on the first coach and being responsible for return loadings — not something covered in the PSV driving test. Loading for the outward journey was the responsibility of staff at the main joining points. Such a complex operation was helped no end by using the same hired coaches and experienced regular drivers. Stephen Barber recalls that Smith's of Thirsk was a regular SFB contributor and that two of its drivers were brothers who, from Monday to Friday, were farmers. Paul Heywood, during his driving days, remembers one busy summer Saturday when seemingly every coach within a 100-mile radius was on the road, and he had to collect a party arriving by plane at Yeadon airport and take them to The Calls. The only vehicle available was a Daimler double-decker of (WA subsidiary) Farsley Omnibus. 'What a let-down for these early jet-setters this must have been,' he muses.

The standing instruction to the Operations staff was that no coach should ever run empty, no matter how great the difference in numbers between outward- and return-journey loadings. Imbalances usually occurred at the start and finish of local holiday weeks. Fortunately those of neighbouring towns did not overlap, so close contact was maintained with nearby operators so as to utilise any single journeys they might have to make up a well-loaded round trip. Notable in this scheme of things were Yorkshire Traction in Barnsley, Hanson in Huddersfield and Hebble in Halifax.

A flavour of what it was like to travel on a WA express is provided by the memories of Perry Cliff, a transport enthusiast from Otley, as recorded in the *Yorkshire Evening Post*. During the 1950s his family regularly travelled by WA coach to Blackpool to visit his grandparents, booking tickets at Mr Waye's travel office at 56 Kirkgate. 'By 1955 I often made the journey on my own, it being considered a natural progression for a seven-year-old. I had a very small suitcase containing all the essentials — notebook, map, timetables,

postcards, photographs, diary and a selection of Dinky Toys,' he remembers. 'There were no major roads until the Preston by-pass was built in 1958, and the journey was an adventure. Continues Perry: 'We travelled on winding roads and undulations, giving glimpses of Wharfdale, Craven, Pendle, Bowland and Ribble. I recorded every settlement we passed through.' Unfortunately he was not a good traveller, recalling: 'The coaches made unscheduled stops for me.' By Guisburn he was able to partake of his rations — a bottle of soda water and a pack of cheese biscuits — whilst the coach took a 15min break at the Commercial Hotel. Having recovered by Lytham, he was ready to be the first to spot the Tower and will, he continues, 'never forget the excitement of the final run through the sand hills and seeing the trams at Starr Gate'. The whole thing took four hours and was, he concludes, 'a great time for a lad'.

As with excursions, the express programme declined and was ultimately sold to a company set up by a former WA manager. Attempts by WA in 1986 to offer a joint express programme with West Yorkshire PTE were not successful, and involvement in this market ceased shortly thereafter.

Above: Delivered in 1953 was a solitary AEC Regal IV with Plaxton Venturer body. Plaxton also bodied six Bedfords, thus becoming second to Burlingham as WA's preferred supplier. It would soon overtake it, and in the late-1950s become WA's first choice. Here RUG 294, well labelled but with an incorrect destination blind, waits at Blackpool to return on an express service to Leeds. Maybe Perry Cliff was a passenger that day. *Stephen Barber collection*

Above: Two of the 1970 deliveries based at Castleford depot. These were part of a batch of 53-seat Plaxton Panorama Elite-bodied Leyland Leopards hired from Stanley Hughes and used on non-tour work. VUB 401H was a regular coach on the South-West Clipper express service from Yorkshire to the West Country, and still displayed the blind despite being on private-hire duty along with its sister. *Stephen Barber collection*

The most popular tour destination was Devon, as confirmed by this brochure extract from 1965: 'On holiday in Devon this year be a Wallace Arnold VIP. Stay in one of the finest hotels with dancing, entertainments and beautiful drives to interesting places. Travel the modern way in a beautiful Wallace Arnold Summer Ivory Limousine Coach, chauffeur-driven with your own specially reserved seat. Relax and be cared for on this loveliest of holidays.' In 1945 WA had bought two hotels in Torquay and subsequently purchased two local coach firms, which became the basis of Wallace Arnold (Devon). In charge was Reg Hele, who had met Robert Barr on a trip to the Netherlands organised by the Dutch Tourist Board. As in so many things, the influence of Robert's contacts is evident. Reg describes him as a 'hands-on man'.

Devon became very much an autonomous unit running its own ship, with booking offices in Torquay and Paignton. Reg built up the business by negotiating the purchase of more coach operators and was justifiably proud of his achievement. From 12 in 1949, there were, by 1959, just two operators in Torquay — WA and Devon General's Grey Cars. There was fierce competition between the two, but Reg feels Grey Cars went downhill after Devon General's sale to the National Bus Company in 1969, following which Grey Cars was amalgamated with another former BET coach operator, Greenslades of Exeter. The new management did not, however, understand the last-minute nature of seaside excursions. 'You could have very few bookings an hour before departure and then, if the weather changed, you'd get six full coaches,' recalls Reg.

POST BRIDGE, DARTMOOR.

See the Delightful West Country with

RUBY AND WAVERLEY TOURS

Early Devon days, when Ruby and Waverley were 'associated with Wallace Arnold'.

Although Devon's autonomy was generally a positive aspect, it also led to some disputes. One year Reg requested Van Hool bodywork for the new coaches, but at the time WA was committed to Plaxton, so that's what came. However, the introduction of the grey livery was something Reg refused to countenance: 'I painted quite enough things grey when I was in the Navy'. Devon coaches stayed ivory, although the fact that Grey Cars' coaches were already painted grey also had something to do with it. Reg puts the Devon subsidiary's success down to three factors. Firstly, there was a great deal of beautiful countryside, so a large and varied excursion package could be offered. Secondly, Devonians were genuinely welcoming and well used to looking after visitors. But key, in Reg's mind, was the 300 miles between Devon and Leeds.

Major Elphee had joined WA in 1955 with the purchase of Feather Bros, of Bradford. As a tour driver he found himself spending up to six months a year in Devon 'on tour', and on his days off he would undertake local excursions for the Devon company. He grew to like it so much that one day he requested a transfer. A telephone call was made to Malcolm Barr, and 10 minutes later it was granted. At the time WA operated out of two depots — one in Seaway Road, Paignton, the other in Babbacombe. The man in charge of the latter was taken ill, and Major was promoted to replace him, finally ending up as Depot Manager for the whole Devon fleet. Eventually a new depot, replacing the other two, was opened in Barton Hill Way, Torquay, where all 28 coaches could be accommodated under cover. Major, who, incidentally, was particularly fond of AECs, spent many hours there and recalls: 'If I was passing and saw a coach outside, I'd stop and put it away.'

Things were very hectic in summer, with a full spread of excursions and a tour programme covering all parts of the country including Scotland and Wales. On occasions there would be eight or nine coaches on a single excursion

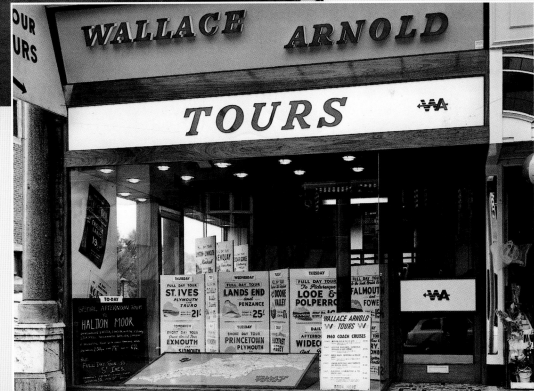

Above and right: Two views of the Torbay Road office in 1960. The traditional advert boards for the various excursions and tours lasted into the 21st century. Note the stylised artwork on the posters, the photograph displayed on the counter and, above it, the painting of a 1958 Plaxton coach — all indicative of local pride in presenting the company.
Stephen Barber (both)

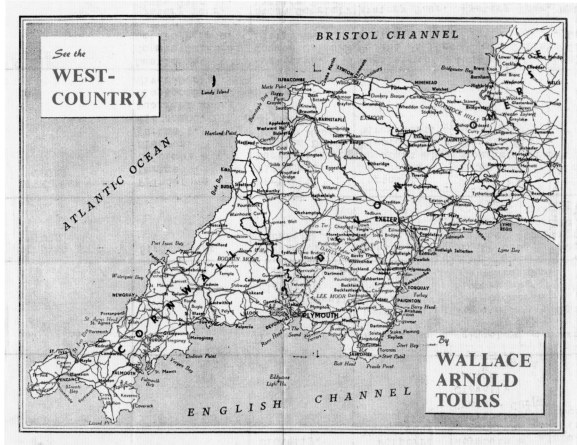

See the
**WEST-
COUNTRY**

By
**WALLACE
ARNOLD
TOURS**

Special Week-end Tours to

LAND'S END & NORTH CORNISH COAST, 2 days: 79/6
ISLES OF SCILLY & LAND'S END, 3 days: 8 Guineas
BOTH TOURS FULLY INCLUSIVE

Horshams Printers Ltd., Paignton.

WALLACE ARNOLD'S

LOCAL EXCURSION

TORQUAY *Booking Offices*

14 Vaughan Road (adjacent Pavilion)	......	Tel.
Belgrave Road	......	Tel. 8
The Kiosk, Castle Circus	......	Tel.
25 Lucius Street	......	Tel.
Hampton Garage, Greenway Road, St. Marychurch	......	Tel. 8
114 Reddenhill Road, Babbacombe	......	Tel. 8
2 Vaughan Road	......	Tel.
149 Reddenhill Road, Babbacombe	......	Tel. 8

PAIGNTON *Booking Offices*

45 Seaway Road, Preston	......	Tel. 8
7 Torbay Road	......	Tel. 5
16 Torbay Road	......	Tel. 5
85 Torbay Road	......	Tel. 5

Above: Local excursions from Devon. Weekly departures were typed on the reverse.

Right: The Devon network.

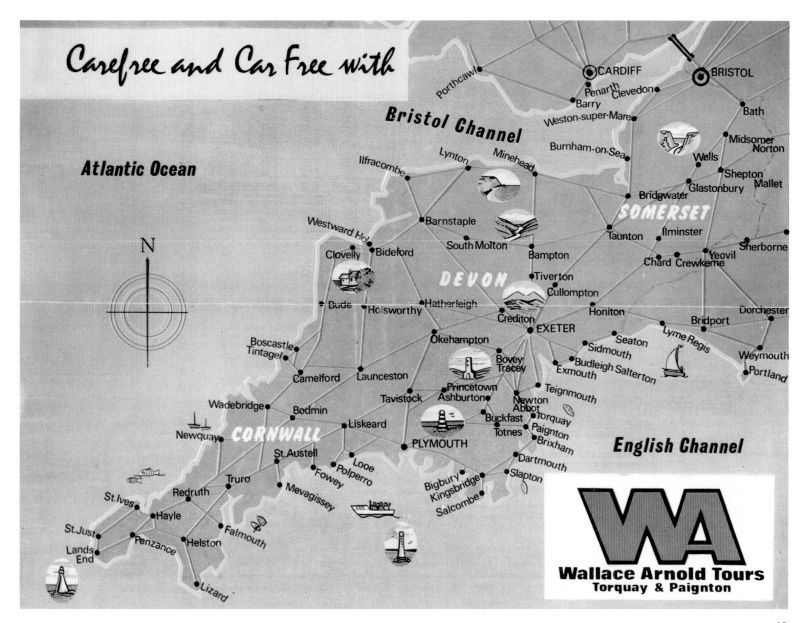

Carefree and Car Free with

Atlantic Ocean

Bristol Channel

English Channel

CORNWALL

DEVON

SOMERSET

N

Porthcawl
CARDIFF
BRISTOL
Penarth Clevedon
Barry
Weston-super-Mare
Bath
Burnham-on-Sea
Midsomer Norton
Wells
Shepton Mallet
Glastonbury
Bridgwater
Ilminster
Sherborne
Taunton
Yeovil
Chard Crewkerne
Dorchester
Bridport
Lyme Regis
Weymouth
Portland

Lynton Minehead
Ilfracombe
Barnstaple
South Molton
Bampton
Tiverton
Cullompton
Westward Ho!
Clovelly Bideford
Hatherleigh
Honiton
Bude Holsworthy
Crediton
EXETER
Seaton
Sidmouth
Boscastle
Tintagel
Okehampton
Bovey Tracey
Budleigh Salterton
Exmouth
Camelford Launceston
Princetown
Ashburton
Teignmouth
Wadebridge
Tavistock
Newton Abbot
Torquay
Bodmin
Buckfast
Paignton
Newquay
Liskeard
PLYMOUTH
Totnes
Brixham
St.Austell
Looe
Dartmouth
Truro
Fowey Polperro
Slapton
Redruth
Mevagissey
Bigbury
Kingsbridge
St.Ives
Hayle
Salcombe
St.Just
Penzance Helston
Falmouth
Lands End
Lizard

WA
Wallace Arnold Tours
Torquay & Paignton

departure. However, it was very quiet in winter, and drivers had to be laid off. Major recalls them being a good group and feeling 'upset when I had to do that'. Usually, however, the same drivers would return for the next season. Winter was a time for maintenance: Major further recalls scraping the underside of coaches with a blow-lamp — 'a filthy job' — and being delighted that the new depot sported a steam-cleaning plant. He felt the company was very much a part of the Devon scene, not least with its distinctive narrow (7ft 6in) coaches, needed to negotiate bridges on Dartmoor.

Sometimes the autonomy was a bit strong. As we have seen earlier, a coach operating on, say, an excursion for which WA had no licence had to run 'on hire' to an operator that did. This applied to WA coaches from Leeds running local excursions in Devon as part of a tour. It was normal for WA Devon to charge WA Leeds for this privilege, for many years the fee being £10. Given that fares — for example, for the

ever-popular excursion to Buckfast Abbey (beware of the tonic wine) — were around 5s 6d (27p), this was a sizeable sum. One year WA Devon decided to put its fee up to £12, so, failing to get special treatment, WA Leeds got a quote of £10 from arch rival Grey Cars.

Reg's view had basis. Stephen Barber remembers his first contact with Reg in Devon, when a Leeds driver needed a replacement coach for the following day. Stephen advised him to pop into the depot and get one. A little later his phone rang, the conversation going as follows.

Reg Hele (irate): "Do you know what day it is tomorrow?"

Stephen Barber: "Wednesday."

Reg Hele (even more irate): "It's Widdecombe Fair — every coach for miles is booked!"

Stephen is embarrassed to admit that until then he thought the Fair existed only in the folk-song. Devon was an interesting and individual part of the empire.

Right: A varied line-up of Devon coaches in Exeter in 1963 on excursions from Torquay and Paignton. 4325 UA is a 1959 Duple Britannia-bodied AEC Reliance, 2648 NW a 1958 Plaxton Consort-bodied Reliance — both 8ft wide. However, 79 BUA, a 1962 Reliance with Plaxton Embassy bodywork, looks wider than its 7ft 6in. *Stephen Barber collection*

Right: A typical Devon coach — a narrow Plaxton Panorama-bodied AEC Reliance dating from 1967. It has the new WA logo, but retains the ivory livery to avoid confusion with Grey Cars. JUA 315E was one of three identical vehicles; they were the last centre-door vehicles and the last AEC Reliances that were purchased not leased, marking the end of two significant chapters in WA's history. *Andrew Wiltshire collection*

Left: The Devon operation was boosted in 1974 by the purchase of the Embankment Motor Co of Plymouth. It brought tour and excursion licences as well as a fleet of Bedford coaches, the newest of which was UJY 58L, a 1973 Bedford YRT/Duple Dominant, seen in full WA livery but with Embankment fleetnames. *John Whitmore / Stuart Jones collection*

Right: In 1975 six Bristol LH coaches were ordered for the Devon fleet — perhaps not surprising, given nearby Western National's huge fleet of the things. However, WA drivers found them very unpleasant to drive, and for the engineers they were by far the most unreliable coaches they had. Three, including HWU 86N, joined the Embankment fleet. Whether their drivers considered them much of an improvement over their Bedford YRQs is not recorded. *Stephen Barber collection*

Left: Devon joined the Duple fold, and this 1977 Leyland Leopard had a rare Dominant body variant owing to its 7ft 8½in width. The windscreens were different sizes. The offside screen, judged by Duple to be the most vulnerable, was the standard size to ease replacement, whereas the nearside one was narrower to compensate for the reduction in the coach's width. SWW 125R has an apparently full and contented load. You might think that it was fitted with a roof board, but that's actually on the office behind. *Stephen Barber collection*

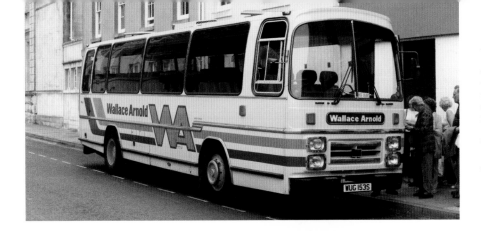

Left: An interesting one-off was this 1978 Leyland Leopard whose original Dominant II body was badly damaged. It was rebodied by Plaxton in its repair shop to the Supreme IV design, and remained unique member in the WA fleet, although further narrow Leopard/Duples would be updated subsequently with Plaxton's Paramount body style.
John Whitmore / Stuart Jones collection

Right: To update its fleet WA (Devon) purchased several late model second-hand Leyland Leopards and Bovas — a rare move for WA. Here one of the Leopards, Plaxton Supreme-bodied YPP 319S, stands alongside a Shearings Ford while operating the very popular Princetown & Plymouth excursion.
Andrew Jarosz / Stephen Barber collection

Left: The Devon fleet was very individual. Proving the point is CKH 454X, a Plaxton Mini Supreme-bodied Mercedes-Benz L608D, formerly a demonstrator. Behind stands a Duple Calypso coach on Bova underframes — one of a batch purchased by Parks of Hamilton that had operated under contract to the company in full WA livery before joining the Devon fleet.
John Whitmore / Stuart Jones collection

49

Right: An unusual Plaxton Paramount coach was FUA 376Y, one of a pair of Bedford YMPS 35-seaters purchased in 1983. WA (Devon) saw itself very much as an all-round local coach operator, and vehicles such as this were felt to be attractive to the private-hire market. The presence of the Maidstone & District Leyland Atlantean in the background suggests a visit to a preserved-bus rally.
John Whitmore / Stuart Jones collection

Left: Devon independence. Having already had a request for Van Hool coachwork turned down, Reg Hele had more success later with one for Berkhof, and as a result a number of B10Ms with Berkhof Esprite bodies joined the fleet in the mid-1980s. 724 FAL is shown here at Yeates' yard in Loughborough after disposal. *Stuart Jones*

Right: WA used mini-coaches for feeder services. J764 CWT, a 12-seat Mercedes-Benz 308D in the Devon fleet, is parked outside the travel shop and former Devon head office in Torbay Road, Paignton, having brought passengers to join their excursion coach. Its parking bay is protected by double yellow lines. *Stephen Barber collection*

50

Right: The narrow Duple Dominant-bodied Leopards were rebodied by Plaxton in the mid-1980s, again in the repair shop and not down the line, in view of their non-standard nature. Here Paramount-bodied CSU 936 rounds the seafront at Torquay *en route* to its final excursion pick-up in Paignton. *Stuart Jones*

Left: As the influx of foreign coaches visiting Torbay during the 1980s and 1990s increased there was the growing problem of them getting stuck over the moors on narrow bridges. This was the very reason that WA (Devon) had purchased its fleet of narrow-built coaches. Meetings with concerned councils identified one of the causes was that foreign drivers would follow narrow WA vehicles, relying on their local knowledge. At the first of the narrow bridges the WA coach would 'hop' across and continue on its way whereas the wider coach behind would become jammed. Some form of warning was needed, and narrow Leopard CSU 938 displays such a warning as it makes its way through the outskirts of Torquay. *Stuart Jones*

Regular trips to the Continent started in the 1930s and by the 1950s and '60s were becoming very popular, often giving folk their first taste of foreign travel. Winifred Dockray of Harrogate booked a 12-day 'Four-Country Tour' in August 1958. 'We took a coach to Folkestone, then the ferry to Boulogne, through France to Dunkirk then to Metz, Nancy and Alsace with overnight stops. We had three nights in Innsbruck with trips to smaller places in the Tyrol. It was my first time abroad, and we had plenty of time to see as much as possible, in case we did not have the opportunity to go again.'

Robert's niece, Barbara, was taken on by WA in 1955 and worked in the booking office, which was located in the basement of the Corn Exchange in Leeds. The following year she was promoted to be a courier on Continental holidays. Her first programme was the 'Belgian Coast Tour'. The coach set out from Leeds, and the party spent the night at the Hotel Metropole in Folkestone before taking the ferry to Ostend. The WA coach then made its way up the coast, passing almost door-to-door Moules and Frites restaurants until arriving at the holiday base in Heist-aan-Zee, near Knokke, not far from the Dutch border. In true WA fashion the coach and driver would then disappear with another party, and coach excursions to Brussels, Bruges, Ghent and the like were undertaken using Belgian operators. Barbara would then return with the party to Folkestone,

where she would collect the next party and head back to Belgium, returning to Leeds only at the end of the season. The following year she was promoted to a Swiss tour — an entirely different affair staying at the five-star Hotel Jungfrau in Interlaken; on this tour the WA driver and coach stayed with the party. It was on one of her visits to Folkestone that she first met Francis Flin, from Croydon, whose job it was to look after the administration of Continental tours. In 1958 they married — 'truly a marriage of coach operators,' says Barbara — and after two more seasons she retired to start a family.

But it didn't end there. Barbara's mentor at WA was one Mary Laycock, who subsequently emigrated to New Zealand. It was Mary who, having suffered a coach breakdown while *en route* to Switzerland, found a railway signalbox and got the signalman to stop the next train to Dijon to take her passengers onwards, so she was clearly not someone to turn down a challenge; she also appeared in one of the promotional films produced by WA. Returning to Leeds from New Zealand

Right: When WA returned to Burlingham in 1953 the Seagull had acquired an additional side moulding as seen here. Not to many people's taste, it was soon deleted, and the following year's deliveries reverted to the previous sleek appearance. RUA 293 was one of a batch of seven Royal Tigers which when new were used on European tours. Mary Laycock would have spent much of her working day sat on the front seat. By 1958, when this photograph was taken, RUA 293 had forsaken Switzerland for more mundane work and is seen in Bradford about to head off on an excursion. *John Cockshott / Stephen Barber collection*

in 1977, Mary was asked to take on a Swiss tour, which, despite having been away for nine years, she did. However, visa restrictions meant that she could not be out of New Zealand for more than six months, so she asked Barbara if she would take on the rest of the programme. With her family's backing she did, and stayed for another seven years. By now things had changed. The crossing was by hovercraft, the party being taken on by a French or Belgian coach; then, at the border, a Swiss coach would take over. On 14-day tours Barbara would return to Leeds and go back to Switzerland almost straight away; on 12-day tours she at least got two days at home. As previously, she found the clients 'the most delightful people, who were so thrilled to be going abroad'. She felt that WA attracted a 'really nice type of person', and this was reflected in the staff, all of whom were extremely loyal. The drivers she recalls as 'top class, very smart and a cut above the rest'. Her regular driver at one time was Tom Whinn, who, when staying at a hotel, would change his driver's blazer for a suit, prompting passengers to remark that he looked as if he owned the establishment.

Tours were always enlivened by one joker who kept everyone laughing. During the late 1970s, on one tour based in Weggis, near Lucerne, a day trip to Grindelwald included a stop at a small chairlift, where passengers sat side-by-side. A young couple, on returning to the coach, announced that during the trip they had become engaged. On the next tour, as the coach pulled up at the chairlift, Barbara announced that this was a romantic trip, and related the tale of the young couple. From the back of the coach came a deep Yorkshire voice: "Cans't tha' get a divorce too?" Barbara thought it was a wonderful job. 'I loved it,' she said, 'and was loath to retire.'

Much more out of the ordinary, but typical of WA's connection with the public mood, a coach packed with relief supplies was sent to Hungary after the Revolution in 1956. As journalist John Morgan of the *Yorkshire Evening Post* noted in 1997, 'The firm, which started in Leeds, rose from modest Sunday-school outings to excursions to all parts of the Continent. Such expansion is remarkable, and WA's distinctive coaches are a familiar sight in all parts of Europe.'

Above: WA was growing its European network in the late 1970s and early 1980s, entrusting the work to a batch of 12m Plaxton-bodied Volvo B58s fitted with 'Bristol domes', so called because of their initial introduction on bodies fitted to Bristol chassis, the front-mounted radiator of which precluded the incorporation of the destination screen beneath the windscreen. Having returned from Rome, EWW 235T awaits servicing at Gelderd Road.
Andrew Jarosz / Stephen Barber collection

Right: Spellbinding holidays abroad in 1960; note the fashion of the times.

Far right: The 1963 purchase of Hallen Coaches in Bristol opened this important market. Here's the Continental brochure for 1965.

HOLIDAYS are Golden days with Wallace Arnold 1960

Spellbinding Holidays Abroad

1965 CONTINENTAL HOLIDAYS from BRISTOL by Wallace Arnold

9. BUS STOP

Although known as a coach operator, WA also had significant bus operations. First came the acquisition in 1952 of Hardwicks of Scarborough, consolidating WA's presence in the town's coach market. It brought with it a bus route to Ebberston. Such was its success that WA invested in a new Leyland PD2 double-decker for use on the service. Hardwicks' manager, George Alden, had an office in the town's bus station. George brought eggs into work which he sold to staff and customers alike. This was a traditional rural bus service, popular with its regulars — all of whom were known to the conductors, who would ask after the well-being of those temporarily missing. In later years Malcolm Barr was to comment that he thought it an ideal bus operation.

Also in 1952 Farsley Omnibus, based in Stanningley and running a suburban route between Pudsey and Horsforth, west of Leeds, joined the group. Finally, in 1956, on the other side of Leeds, the Kippax & District fleet, running to Garforth and Kippax, was purchased. As with all other operations, all of this work was in competition with other operators.

On the Scarborough route Hardwicks competed with state-owned United Automobile Services, which ran to Pickering and Ripon, although regulars let 'the United' go by. Services in Leeds were hotly contested by Leeds City Transport. An attempt by WA to extend operations into a new estate near Horsforth resulted in an objection by LCT, instigated by its Traffic Manager, Arnold Stone, and leading to a lengthy traffic court battle that WA ultimately lost. On the other side of the city, the lucrative Ninelands Estate in Garforth was a good money-spinner; here competition was provided by the independent West Riding Automobile Co, based in Wakefield. Paul Heywood remembers being sent during quieter winter months to monitor the activities of West Riding to check that it was not illegally carrying Kippax passengers during the peak. In effect Kippax & District buses ran limited-stop within Leeds, with their own stops outside the city boundary.

WA was not impressed by the proposed introduction of the Passenger Transport Executives, as outlined in the Transport Act 1968, and feared compulsory purchase. Anticipating a better deal from a voluntary sale, WA sold its Leeds bus operations to LCT in March 1968 — something Malcolm Barr always regretted. The Scarborough route survived and expanded after deregulation in 1986, but the management team felt that it was not part of the core business of the company and in 1987 sold it to Hull-based East Yorkshire Motor Services.

FARSLEY OMNIBUS COMPANY
Telephone Stanningley 71983
Proprietor MAURICE GREENWOOD

TIME TABLE
OF SERVICE

STANNINGLEY
(SUNFIELD)
—TO—
HORSFORTH
(COUNCIL OFFICES)
VIA
FARSLEY and RODLEY

West Riding ABC Publishing Co., Ltd., Stanningley

A Farsley Omnibus timetable from before WA days when it was run by proprietor Maurice Greenwood.

Left: The Hardwicks fleet, purchased by Wallace Arnold in 1952, was a typical country-bus mix of Bedford buses and coaches, along with a prewar Dennis Lancet and a 1950 Commer. Things certainly changed under the new owners with the arrival in 1953 of this splendid new Leyland PD2, seen in the smart fleet livery. Withdrawn from service in 1967, this classic bus went for scrap, having succumbed to a cracked chassis. *Stephen Barber collection*

Left: Good housekeeping around the Hunslet Road workshops seems lacking as AUM 433 stands surrounded by scrap metal. The well-signed (but hidden) stores is decidedly at the lower end of the market, and a far cry from Eric Stockwell's days as Chief Engineer. New to Leeds City Transport in 1935, this AEC Regent had its Roe body rebuilt by East Lancs (Bridlington) in 1947/8. Purchased by Wallace Arnold in June 1951, it joined the newly acquired Hardwicks Services in 1952 and was sold in 1956 to a showman in the South of England. *Stephen Barber collection*

Left: Another acquisition from Leeds City Transport was this 1936 Leyland TD4 with classic Roe bodywork. Purchased in 1950 and used at Royston depot on works contracts, it moved to greener pastures at Hardwicks in 1952. It returned to Leeds in 1954 and spent its final days with Farsley Omnibus, where it is seen here at a still recognisable Stanningley Bottom *en route* from Pudsey to Horsforth. It was withdrawn in 1956. *Colin Routh / Stephen Barber collection*

Right: Farsley Omnibus had been acquired in October 1952. The fleet consisted of four Roe-bodied Daimler CVD6 single-deckers, three of which are seen parked outside the WA depot at Hunslet Road. They had been replaced by double-deckers in 1956 and transferred to the main fleet for contract work. Visible in the background, on layover after working a weekend troop service, is a Harrington-bodied Leyland Tiger Cub belonging to Silver Star of Porton Down — one of many operators involved in such work in the 1950s and '60s. Vehicles would arrive late on a Friday night and be purloined by WA for a full day's work on Saturday before returning south on Sunday. *John Cockshott / Stephen Barber collection*

Right: MUM 461 entered WA service in 1950 as a Wilks & Meade-bodied coach. Along with three similar vehicles, it was transferred to Farsley Omnibus in 1954 to augment the fleet. All four were rebodied as double-deckers by Roe in 1956; three, including this example returning to Farsley, the fourth going to Hardwicks. MUM 461, seen here in Pudsey when newly rebodied, has drawn a small crowd to view the strange stepped platform which was a distinctive feature of these buses. It ended its days with Kippax Motors, its eventful career drawing to a close in 1968. *Stephen Barber collection*

Right: From one iconic fleet to another. ARN 185 was originally with Ribble and was a 1947 Burlingham-bodied Leyland PD1 purchased in 1958 as a spare vehicle for the stage-carriage fleets. It is seen here parked in Leeds bus station bearing the Kippax Motors fleetname but displaying a rare Farsley Omnibus short-working destination. Leeds 472 beside it shows off that fleet's signature silver bonnet. The building behind can still be seen today. *Stephen Barber collection*

Left: Kippax Motors, purchased in 1956, brought with it some prewar classics, including BWR 98, a 1935 all-Leyland TD4, which was withdrawn by WA the following year. Also visible in this view at Hunslet Road are two other exiles from acquired fleets — a Farsley Daimler CVD6 and HKW 240, a Feather Bros AEC Regal IV. *John Cockshott / Stephen Barber collection*

Left: WA updated its bus fleet with rebodied Daimler and new Leyland double-deckers. The Kippax route was the busiest and most profitable, receiving the first PD3 in 1960. Roe-bodied 6237 UB, seen here heading to Garforth, is trying to keep up with a striding man who studiously ignores its presence. It stayed at Kippax until the end in 1968 before crossing the Irish Sea to work for the Londonderry & Lough Swilly Railway Co.
Stephen Barber collection

Right: One of four famous (or infamous) AEC Swifts with Park Royal bodies purchased from Sheffield City Transport in 1971. Sadly for such smart buses, they were unreliable and were withdrawn after only three years' service, as they had been in Sheffield. The vehicles were sold by tender, and when the WA team went to collect them from Sheffield, TWE 23F wouldn't start, so 28 was taken instead. It was an omen. The four refused to start on numerous occasions — usually when in service. TWE 28F is seen here at Gelderd Road in Hardwicks' version of the grey livery.
Andrew Wiltshire collection

Left: Two former Southdown Leyland PD3 'Queen Mary' double-deckers were purchased for publicity purposes. 'Uncle Wally' lived in Torquay and operated sightseeing tours around Torbay, although he is seen here passing the imposing Leeds City Hall ahead of a West Yorkshire PTE Access Express. 'Uncle Arnold' was based in Leeds. Both were used in parades and to celebrate sporting success by any local team.
Stephen Barber collection

Above: Occasionally the 'Queen Marys' went further afield — notably, as illustrated here, to the 1998 ABTA Convention in Marbella. It is testimony to the Leyland product of their day that the journeys to and from Spain were completed without any mechanical problems.
Stephen Barber

Conveying the scale and diversity of WA's operations is something of a challenge, but some impression can be gleaned from the 1975 financial results, contained in a report entitled 'How are we doing at Barr & Wallace Arnold Trust Ltd?' Issued to all employees in September 1976, this was followed up by meetings in Leeds, London, Edinburgh and Torquay, to which all staff were invited. Malcolm Barr advises that the purpose of this exercise was threefold — firstly to give information about the group, secondly to set out the directors' views about the group's approach to business, and thirdly to help employees understand the relationship of the group to the wider commercial scene, including 'why we do, and sometimes have to do, certain things'.

At that time the group consisted of three divisions — Holiday, Motor and Computer Bureau. Staff numbers totalled

1,467, working from 69 locations and earning a gross profit of £905,063. This was put into context. Sales realised £28,275,000, while costs amounted to £27,370,000, resulting in a profit of just 3% of total sales. Put another way, for every £100 worth of sales, costs amounted to £96.80, resulting in a profit of £3.20. Of the gross profit 52% was payable as Corporation Tax, leaving a final net profit of £412,187.

The Computer Bureau, established in 1964, had subsidiaries in Leeds, Sale (Manchester) and Birmingham, whilst the Motor division's subsidiaries amounted to six in Leeds (including Wilks & Meade), two in Bradford and one in Nottingham. But for our tour we are more interested in the Holidays division. This operated from 52 locations, employed 869 people and provided £492,161 of the gross profit. It was responsible for the provision of inclusive holiday tours, the

Below: In the 1950s the British Safety Council produced a booklet on advanced driving, with a foreword by its National Director, Leonard D. Hodge. It must have been produced in regional editions, as this advert for 'Wallace Arnold — The Coach Firm' shows.

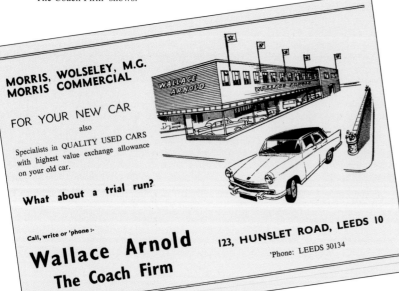

MORRIS, WOLSELEY, M.G. MORRIS COMMERCIAL

FOR YOUR NEW CAR
also
Specialists in QUALITY USED CARS with highest value exchange allowance on your old car.

What about a trial run?

Call, write or 'phone :-

Wallace Arnold 123, HUNSLET ROAD, LEEDS 10
The Coach Firm 'Phone: LEEDS 30134

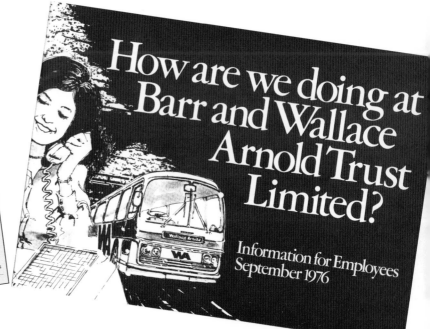

How are we doing at Barr and Wallace Arnold Trust Limited?

Information for Employees September 1976

Right: Duple's influence grew, and in 1976 it achieved its ambition of supplying the entire WA order. Among the vehicles were four 12m Leyland Leopards including NNW 108P seen here when new on a Torquay tour. These 1976 WA deliveries had prototype framework in preparation for the revamped Dominant II in 1976. Note the flat lower side panels compared with HWU 73N. *Stephen Barber collection*

Left: Four of the distinctive 1977 Dominant IIs were built to an enhanced specification including reclining seats and trimmed in *avant garde* striped moquette. Here, almost new SWW 148R is seen operating the company's flagship British tour, the 14-day 'Glory of Highland Scotland'. *Stephen Barber collection*

Left: While Duple continued to enjoy the bulk of the WA order, 1978 saw the arrival of six Plaxton Supreme-bodied Volvo B58s, the full significance of which was not fully appreciated at the time. Two of the Volvos were 12m-long, and, surprisingly, were allocated to Evan Evans. XWX 201S is seen on a London sightseeing tour. *Andrew Jarosz / Stephen Barber collection*

Right: For 1979 the order was shared between Leyland and Volvo and indeed between Duple and Plaxton. Here Duple Dominant II-bodied Leyland Leopard EWW 217T, during the course of a West Country tour, stands next to the old enemy — a Shearings Plaxton Supreme-bodied Ford R1114. The coach is in a revised livery suggested by Duple, which does not do the design much justice. A sign of overheating problems at that period with the Leopard chassis is the moving of the numberplate to allow more air to reach the radiator.
Stephen Barber collection

Right: An identical Duple body, but on a Volvo B58 chassis, stands at The Calls in Leeds prior to departing on an excursion. The advertising boards in the background lack the attraction of earlier years, and things at The Calls are beginning to go downhill. Although WA was closely involved with testing components for Leyland's forthcoming Tiger the manufacturer did not seem to recognise this, and Leyland's mishandling of WA's large Tiger order for 1980 brought to an end a relationship that had lasted over 50 years. Henceforth the Swedish invasion could not be halted. A sad reflection indeed on the UK bus- and coach-building industry at that time.
Tony Greaves / Steven Barber collection

Right: Reg Hele chose to remain with the Leopard chassis for the Devon fleet but reverted to Plaxton coachwork with an attractive new livery style and increased interior specification. Here Supreme IV-bodied EWW 205T unloads its tour passengers, suitably clad for a damp day, at Exeter coach station. In the background are a mixture of Devon General and former Exeter City buses during the short-lived time when red livery was used for both.
Stephen Barber collection

Notwithstanding Malcolm Barr's upbeat message in the 1976 report, this was, in many ways, a tough time for WA. It experienced increasing battles for market share, suffering badly, especially in its Yorkshire heartland and in particular with Lancashire-based Smiths-Happiways-Spencers and with Shearings-Pleasureways-Ribblesdale. WA's traditional policies of intensive vehicle operation and maximum profit generation were letting it down. Customers' needs were increasingly coming second to vehicle efficiency, and the prices charged were leading to high expectations that were not met, resulting in a growth of complaints. A former WA Managing Director, John King, remembers that the company, always wanting to generate as much income as possible from a tour, worked on a revenue balance of a 50/50 share of the fare between hotel costs and travel costs. He feels it would have been better to settle for a 40% share for travel.

There was small comfort in the fact that the fledgling National Bus Company, formed in 1969, was, bluntly, making a mess of amalgamating the long-established tour operations of its constituent companies. For a while others benefited from this, but by around 1980 NBC had got its act together in a big way, helped by the fact that it had recruited former WA management. National Holidays, as the division was known, soon became a respected name and was particularly successful in the South East of England. How, you ask, could this have been a threat to Leeds-based Wallace Arnold? Well, the stark reality was that, since the early postwar years, London and the South East had constituted WA's largest market, bigger even than its Yorkshire homeland.

The deregulation of coach services in 1980 meant that the complex licensing arrangements of the preceding five decades were swept away, and entry into the market became much easier. WA hoped to benefit from this and was a founder member of the British Coachways venture — a doomed attempt to take on the National Express network, from which it withdrew after a mere 12 months. Further attempts were made to run express coaches from Leeds to London, but WA finally ended up working for National Express — something that didn't sit too comfortably.

Other initiatives were tried. 'InTent', for example, was an attempt to capture the camping market, while 'Go Bananas' was a shot at the youth market, travelling to European hotspots. If they didn't work — and most didn't — they were ruthlessly shut down. So too were the company's depots. Those at Castleford, Royston, Bradford and Pudsey were all closed, all coaches now being based at Leeds. The London-based Evan Evans company, acquired in 1969 but never a happy fit (and into which WA poured a fortune), was finally sold in 1984, as was the ground-breaking Northern Computer Bureau. Things looked bleak, but Chairman Malcolm Barr was not prepared to see the business go under and rejected a bid from its Lancashire rivals, now merged as Smiths-Shearings and owned by Pleasurama. His solution was delightfully simple: recruit the old WA team back from National Holidays — which is what, in 1985, he did.

The new team was headed by John King as Managing Director and included Stephen Barber as Operations Director, both originally WA men, and, with their colleagues, they entirely changed the company, breathing new life into it. The team first turned its attention to the fleet, seeking the advice of long-standing and well-respected WA Engineer Eric Stockwell. He was clear: the best product for WA's needs was the Volvo/Plaxton combination. At the time WA had options on a bewildering array of types, but these were cancelled, and a long-standing, largely successful relationship was started.

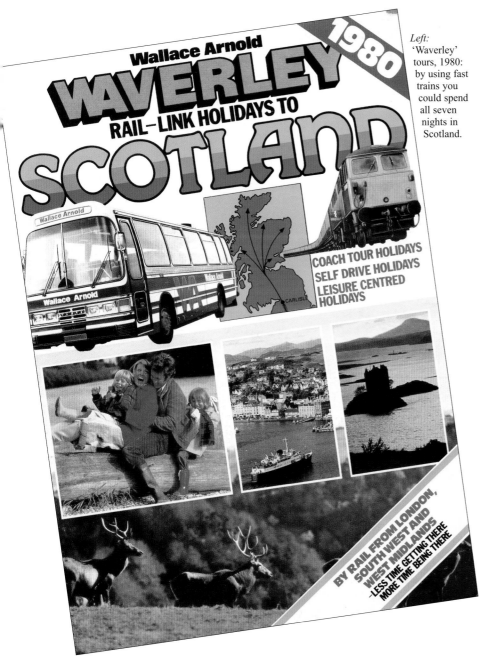

Left:
'Waverley'
tours, 1980:
by using fast
trains you
could spend
all seven
nights in
Scotland.

Eric was a legendary engineer with strongly held views; he believed an auxiliary coach-heating system should be independent of the engine. As such he favoured the unusual air-operated Webasto, rather than the more usual water-operated system. Subsequently a body order was placed with Van Hool, which was unfamiliar with air-operated Webasto heaters but, in its usual way, got on and fitted them. Eric's engineering skills were a key part of WA's success.

It was decided that the way forward was to change the company from being a coach operator into a holiday company that happened to use its own coaches. Out went the vehicle-dominated programmes, and tours started to cater more for customer needs, coaches on the main scenic tours staying with their respective driver and passengers. Previously

Right: From
the late
1970s WA
was
involved
with
Euroways.

Left: The wonders of King's Cross Coach Station and the delights of British Coachways come together in this shot of a 1980 12m Volvo B58/Plaxton Supreme IV awaiting departure from what was essentially a glorified bombsite.
Andrew Wiltshire collection

Left: Against the majestic background of St Pancras Buildings, now home to Eurostar train services, Volvo/Plaxton LUA 255V heads towards the 'bombsite' to pick up its passengers in 1981. Not realised at the time, the Volvo years had arrived.
Stephen Barber collection

Right: British Coachways and Birmingham. Resplendent in full British Coachways livery, 12m Leopard/Plaxton LUA 285V of the Devon fleet prepares to leave the short-lived WA coach station in Park Street for Torquay. *Stephen Barber collection*

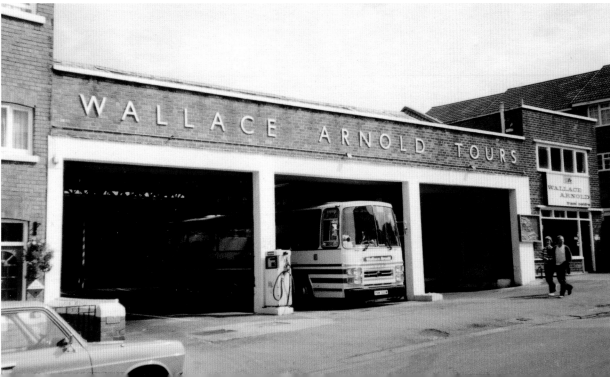

Left: Columbus Ravine, WA's Scarborough base, the depot empty apart from PNW 320W. This coach was from the two large batches of Plaxton-bodied Ford R1114s delivered in 1980 and 1981 for private-hire and excursion work. *Stuart Jones*

Right: Although it had been very involved in pre-production work on the Leyland Tiger chassis, when it came to deliveries WA felt it was a long way down the list of customers. Three initial vehicles with different specifications to assess the alternatives for future orders were months late, and the 1981 order had to be substituted with Leopards. It was a bad move on Leyland's part, and WA looked elsewhere for its chassis from then on. Here is one of the three late Tigers at Gelderd Road. Like the other two, VWX 295X had a Plaxton Supreme IV GT body. *Andrew Jarosz / Stephen Barber collection*

Right: Even more surprising was the purchase of four Kässbohrer Setra S215Hs, which, although far in advance of a Plaxton-bodied Leopard, suffered from driver abuse. A powerful rear engine, manual gearbox and a rev counter were a very different driving experience from semi-automatic Leopards and Volvos. Here are the four 1982 Setras, newly arrived at Gelderd Road. *Stephen Barber collection*

Left: After a large but traditional intake in 1981 — including the unwanted Leopards — 1982 saw a complete change in coach buying. WA became the first large UK customer for the Bova Europa, one of which, VWX 357X, is seen on demonstration at the Blackpool Coach Rally. Supplied by Alf Moseley, it still carries the dealer's trade plates. *Stuart Jones*

Left: 1983 saw the arrival of more Bovas — the last to be purchased new. One of the virtues of the Europa was its price, but its replacement the Futura cost the same as a Plaxton-bodied Volvo B10M, and for WA there was no advantage. Bova shared the 1983 order with a large batch of coaches sporting the new-generation Plaxton Paramount body on Volvo B10M chassis, which was to become the Wallace Arnold standard until 1992. Here is one of the final Bovas, FUA 404Y, passing WA's original head office as it enters the coach station in The Calls. *Stephen Barber*

71

they had not, being inter-worked to get, theoretically, the most efficient vehicle usage. Departures and returns were spread over Fridays to Mondays, and private hires and excursions, the latter market in any case in steep decline, were undertaken only on Tuesday, Wednesday and Thursday — traditionally quiet tour days. An attempt was made to encourage prospective excursion customers to leave their cars at Gelderd Road and join the coach there, rather than Leeds city centre. One leaflet had a misprint which read: 'leave your cat at Gelderd Road' — which caused Terry Wogan much amusement when a listener to his BBC Radio 2 breakfast show sent him a copy. For excursions the writing was, however, on the wall.

As for coach tours, in the past people had been willing to, say, catch a train from the South Coast to join a WA coach tour at their traditional starting point in Croydon or at King's Cross. This was no longer acceptable, so complex and costly feeders had to be provided to meet customers' higher expectations. Coaches now had to go to the people, not the other way around. Hotels needed more facilities, and centred holidays became more popular, as holidaymakers did not want to be changing hotels every night. Post 1985 the firm began to purchase hotels and travel shops, ending up with nine of the former and 24 of the latter, becoming much more a holiday company. The logic behind this policy was that if WA covered all aspects of the holiday it could control the quality of the whole package.

Under the terms of the Transport Act 1985 all NBC companies were to be sold, and National Holidays became the first, going to the Pleasurama Group, which also owned Lancashire-based Shearings. By 1990 the group — to WA's amazement and delight — had decided to drop the National Holidays name in favour of Shearings, a name completely unknown in the key South East market. Much of the market was virtually handed over on a plate, and WA moved from steady growth to suddenly surging ahead.

Left: Autumn and Spring Breaks 1988/9, featuring a rare Volvo C10M.

WA **Wallace Arnold**

BRITISH BREAKS
AUTUMN & SPRING

ALSO INCLUDING HOLIDAYS TO JERSEY, GRANADA TV STUDIO TOURS, ACTIVITY HOLIDAYS, EASTER AND FESTIVE SPECIALS

ABTA 62242

BONDED COACH HOLIDAYS 1988

FREE LOCAL DEPARTURE POINTS

FROM LONDON · SOUTH-EAST · AUTUMN & SPRING

OCT 1988 — APR 1989

AND EAST

WOMAN'S REALM INVITES YOU TO 'THE WORLD OF TELEVISION'

GRANADA STUDIOS AND LUNCH WITH A STAR

SUPER VALUE WEEKEND BREAK FEBRUARY — APRIL 1989

ONLY £85 PER PERSON

WA was allowed access to the Granada Studios to set up a programme with the magazine *Woman's Realm* for 1989. Note Stephen Barber delivering Newton & Ridleys to the Rovers. WA was sponsor of the Granada Studios tour.

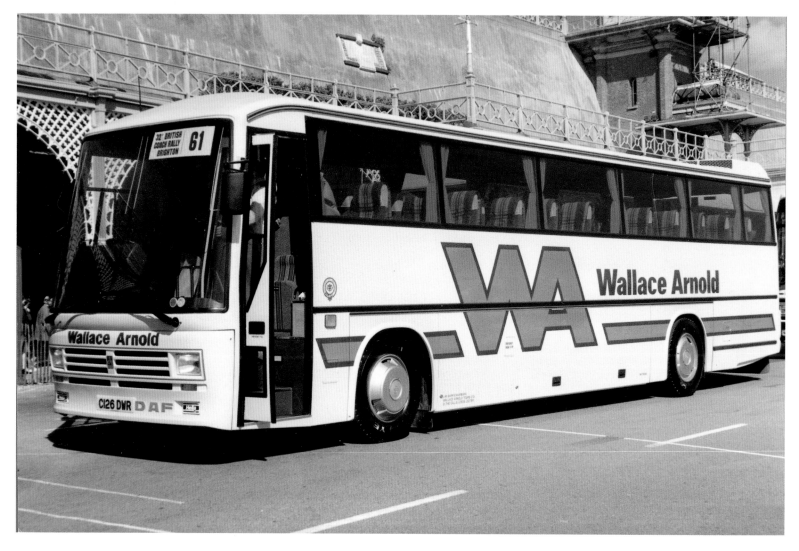

Above and right: To show the outside world it meant business WA's new management entered three vehicles in the 1986 British Coach Rally. One was an example of the then standard Volvo B10M/ Plaxton Paramount combination, the other two being C126 DWR, an early Duple 340-bodied DAF MB230 supplied to the company as a demonstrator, and C158 DWT, a Caetano-bodied Iveco 79.14. On this occasion the travelling rugs were for decoration only, as heating was much improved. *Stuart Jones (both)*

Left: The Volvo C10M integral enjoyed limited success in the UK, and only 10 were imported. WA took the last two in 1987. They were the first air-conditioned coaches in the fleet, but the novel roof-mounted equipment was twice removed by very low bridges. This picture shows one of the type's advantages in terms of increased luggage capacity. *Stuart Jones*

Left: As the 1980s progressed, a number of well-known coach companies came up for sale, unable to cope with the competition let loose by coach deregulation in 1980. WA took advantage and in 1987/8 purchased Cotters, Bee Line and Florence & Grange. Before the operations were integrated with the main WA programme, small numbers of vehicles carried the original names. 9778 WA, a 1985 Plaxton Paramount-bodied Volvo B10M, is branded 'Florence+Grange'. *Andrew Jarosz / Stephen Barber collection*

In 1989 Volvo replaced its faultless Mk II B10M chassis with a less-than-perfect Mk III version. WA reminded Volvo that it expected better by the purchase in 1990 of five Plaxton Paramount III-bodied Mercedes-Benz O.303s. The hint was taken and modifications to the B10M brought it back to the expected standard. Here two of the O.303s are seen at the handover ceremony outside Scarborough. The Mercedes-Benz badges were stuck on with Blu-tack for the photographs. *Plaxton / Stephen Barber collection*

Above: The long association with Plaxton suffered a setback in 1992 following the introduction of a completely new body, the Première, to replace the long-serving Paramount. For that season WA had ordered 63 of the new body off the drawing board, but the result was little short of a disaster, difficulties with new materials, faulty components and certain aspects of the design causing water ingress. The situation was compounded by an abnormally wet spring, and duckboards had to be fitted to keep luggage above the boot floor, which was often waterlogged. The large number of coaches with problems stretched the company's engineering resources to the limit, and the 1993 Plaxton order was cut back to just five vehicles. Here are two new coaches awaiting delivery at Scarborough. Shearings had similar problems with its vehicles and also subsequently gave more business to other builders. *Stuart Jones*

Right: Wallace Arnold turned to Belgium for its 1993 coachwork, and both Van Hool and Jonckheere were delighted to receive orders for 25 and 20 coaches respectively. Both batches of vehicles were of a high standard and gave excellent service. An unregistered Van Hool Alizée is seen posed for photographs outside the factory. *Van Hool / Stuart Jones collection*

Right: Jonckheere Deauville-bodied B10M K828 HUM is seen near Preston picking up its Lancashire passengers travelling to the Scottish Highlands. Stephen Barber's Vauxhall Senator can be seen by the coach. Clearly the Operations Director was on site, but it is not his luggage about to be loaded. *Stephen Barber collection*

Left: Many of the problems with the 1992 Plaxton bodies arose from the large double-hinged boot lid, which was so heavy (and the rams so weak) that it would not stay up. Tightening the rams meant the amount of physical effort to reach up and pull the door down was beyond all but the most physically fit drivers. Across the boot floor, where the lid descended, was a long rubber strip. This was designed to be the waterproof seal, but the weight of the lid flattened the rubber, allowing water to enter. After two years of modifications that did nothing to solve the problem the entire rear end was redesigned, incorporating a conventional boot lid. Here Dennis Javelin GX demonstrator K762 FYG proudly shows what was to become its Achilles heel. To misquote Michael Caine, "You're only supposed to blow the bloody doors off". *Stuart Jones*

Left: The Jonckheere Deauville bodies purchased in the wake of the Plaxton *débâcle* had no such nonsense at the rear. This view at Gelderd Road features Volvo B10M L945 NWW, with its traditional and sensible rear end — hinged door, detachable bumper and a rear window that did not curve into the roof panel. *Stephen Barber collection*

Right: Where it all happens. The driver's seat, not on the usual Volvo B10M but the lone Dennis Javelin GX of 1992. *Stuart Jones*

Left: WA continued to regret the drastic action it had been forced to take regarding Plaxton, and modifications to its product persuaded WA to take an increased number for the 1994 season. Resulting Excalibur-bodied Volvo B10M L928 NWW is seen here operating an Historic Royal Palaces tour from the West Country. *Stephen Barber collection*

Left and below: Jonckheere also received orders for 1995, and two Volvo B10Ms are seen here earning their keep. L960 NWW heads into the sunset while on a tour (dark glasses not provided), while L963 NWW is seen meandering through the picturesque Peak District. *Stuart Jones; Stephen Barber*

Left: More Van Hool Alizée-bodied Volvos were delivered in 1995, this time with the air-conditioning equipment fitted in a less vulnerable position. Unlike the early C10M experiences, none was removed by accident. B10M L906 NWW is seen next to a Scottish Citylink Plaxton Paramount-bodied Leyland Tiger, with its one-man-operated destination blind. *Stuart Jones*

Left: Not the most successful Volvo in the WA fleet was this solitary B6R/Jonckheere of 1994. Seen prior to delivery parked at the Loughborough premises of Volvo dealer Yeates, it was subsequently registered L964 NWW. Giving the impression of being 'over-bodied', it was unpleasant to drive and mechanically unreliable. Its days with WA were limited — parked outside a hotel in Dundee, it was badly damaged when an adjacent car caught fire and was disposed of. *Stuart Jones*

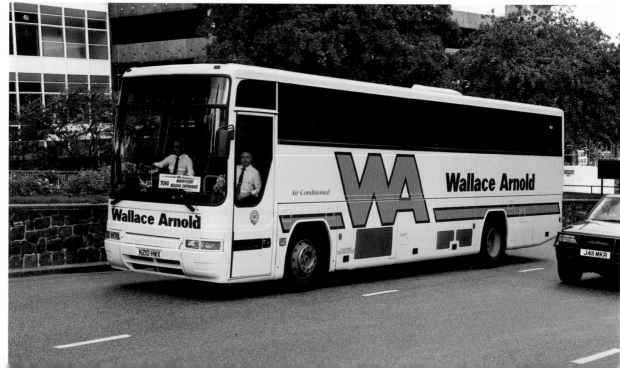

Above: Leeds Rugby League Club (later known as Leeds Rhinos) enjoyed much success in the 1990s. Here coaches for club officials, including the solitary three-axle Volvo B12/ Jonckheere Deauville, are on parade. *Tony Greaves / Stephen Barber collection*

Right: WA's own version of *glasnost*. One of the company's most popular European tours was the 15-day 'Magnificent Russian Experience'. Here Kevin Haigh and Paul Thomas, along with Volvo B10M/Plaxton Première N210 HWX, have returned safely from their trip across Europe in the summer of 1997, with Union flag proudly displayed. *David Cole / Stuart Jones collection*

Above and right: By 1995 Plaxton had retrieved its reputation, and examples of its bodywork once again arrived in large numbers. 'Air Conditioned' M102 UWY is seen operating a Lake Maggiore tour, whilst M118 UWY has paused to sample the delights of Moffat. Both coaches are Première-bodied B10Ms. You pays your money and you takes your choice. *Stuart Jones (both)*

Above: The WA tour operation relied on a network of feeder services and strategically located interchanges. Leicester Forest East, on the M1, was used for passengers from the East and West Midlands to join southbound tour coaches. This 1993 picture shows a mixture of Jonckheere Deauvilles and Plaxton Paramounts and Premières. How many coach operators could have put on a display like this? *Stephen Barber collection*

Right: Volvo B10M/Plaxton Paramount III G501 LWU pulls into Leicester Forest East while on a Great Yarmouth tour. *Stuart Jones*

Gordano Interchange, on the M5 near Bristol, was the hub of WA's South West and South Wales programmes. Here tour coaches gathered at the start and finish of every holiday, passengers being brought in by an extensive feeder network. The practicalities of getting people, luggage and coaches together were daunting. This 1994 photograph shows part of a 15-coach operation, involving more than 500 passengers, being despatched. *Stephen Barber collection*

Right: In 1995 WA holidays linked advertising to a popular TV advert of the time, starring June Whitfield.

As explained earlier, for most of its existence Wallace Arnold Tours was part of the Leeds-based Barr & Wallace Arnold Trust, controlled by the Barr family, the Trust having been set up by company founder Robert Barr in 1937. The Barrs were very influential; indeed, it is no exaggeration to say that they were regarded as a kind of 'Yorkshire royalty'. However, by the mid-1990s the family was divided in its views, so the decision was taken that the business should be split into its two constituent parts — leisure (basically the coach and holiday side) and the motor trade (the vehicle dealerships). The two were to be sold independently, it being advised that the two businesses would be worth more as separate entities.

It was widely anticipated that the leisure side would go to the competing Shearings Holidays business, and indeed there was widespread and persistent speculation to this effect in the local and trade press. However, the successful outcome, in 1997, turned out to be a management buyout backed by venture-capital firm 3i. Shearings later came into the 3i fold too, giving the venture capitalists the opportunity to maximise their investment by merging the two businesses. But this day was still eight years away, and the new order at WA set to with an aim of further strengthening the company.

It was recognised that a modern, high-profile fleet was the key to sustained success. The investment was huge and demanded strict cost control. Maximum coach utilisation was essential, and the reliability of the growing Volvo fleet made this possible. To be part of the fleet a coach had to be guaranteed a minimum of eight months' continuous work. Each WA coach averaged 50,000 miles a year and usually remained in the fleet for three seasons. Revenue from coach sales was considerable, and it was necessary to ensure that the interior specification would be acceptable to prospective purchasers. Coupled with Chief Engineer Eric Stockwell's practical engineering modifications, this meant that there was always a ready market for former WA vehicles — which was just as well, given that there were, on average, 50 coaches annually to be disposed of.

Unlike the bus industry, with its year-in, year-out nature, the coach industry is a one-year-at-a-time operation. At the end of each year the slate is wiped clean, and everything starts again. Once a price was published in the brochure that was it, so accurate budgeting was critical. WA ensured that there would be no nasty surprises by removing as much risk as possible. Regular fleet renewal meant that all coaches operated with a full warranty, and a 'fixed price' fuel contract ensured that whatever happened in the volatile oil market, the company knew the exact cost of its fuel for the next 12 months. Currency fluctuations, which could greatly affect the cost of European hotel accommodation after the brochures had been published for the large WA programme, were minimised by taking out 'currency options' to fix the price of foreign currency in advance. There was much more to running a successful coach-holiday business than owning a few coaches.

In 2001, before the venture capitalists made their move, WA made a particularly significant purchase — that of National Holidays, which had earlier been acquired from Pleasurama by East Yorkshire Motor Services; as explained earlier, by the early 1990s Shearings management felt the name had no value, and it had remained unused for some time before being resurrected by EYMS for its own holiday programme.

In 2002 WA introduced its high-specification 'Grand Tourer' programme, which employed a dedicated fleet of brand-new Volvo coaches. The concept had taken time to develop, and attention to detail was unparalleled. Vehicles were finished in a distinctive livery of black and gold, using BMW paints, while the full-leather interior included a rear coffee lounge with a floral display and a tinted-glass partition inscribed with the company crest. 'GT' registrations were obtained, and drivers wore special uniforms that complemented the livery; even the luggage labels were black and gold. The 'Grand Tourer' programme maintained its own identity, but the lettering gave the assurance of a brand that had become a household name in the eight decades since that meeting in Leeds in 1926 and Robert Barr's momentous decision to keep the name 'Wallace Arnold' — the reason those coaches finishing their day's work in March 2005 still prominently and proudly displayed the orange 'WA' hallmark of excellence.

Left: National Holidays was a major and significant WA acquisition. Retained as a separate entity, it received time-expired WA coaches, although none of the three shown in this 2001 picture came from the WA fleet. *Stuart Jones*

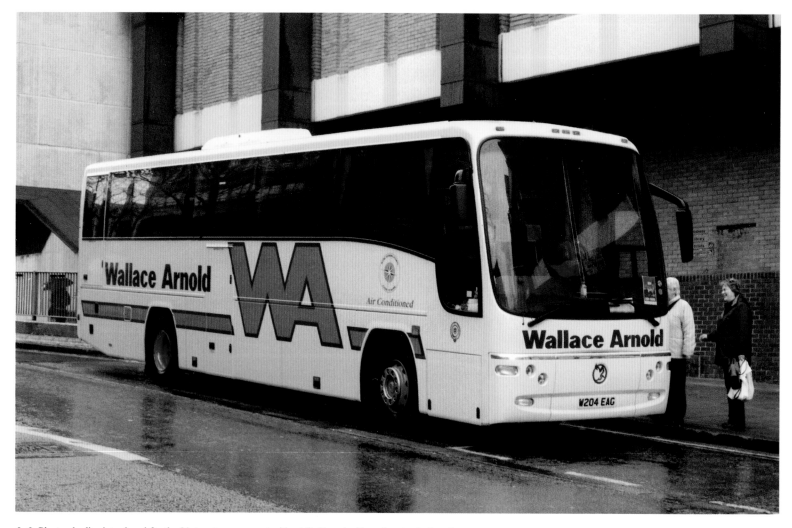

Left: Plaxton bodies introduced for the 21st century were not without faults and, although not as bad as the 1992 product, once again caused WA to look elsewhere for its coachwork. To compound matters the newly acquired National Holidays business added 10 more of these problem vehicles to the fleet. Plaxton Panther-bodied Volvo B10M W204 EAG is seen here repainted in WA livery. *Stuart Jones*

Right: One of WA's own Plaxton Panthers, Volvo B10M X662 NWY, is seen here serving as a team coach for Huddersfield Town FC. *Stephen Barber*

Left: As a result of Plaxton's difficulties Jonckheere bodywork made a return in 2001 in an order shared with Plaxton. The Jonckheere Mistrals, on Volvo B10M chassis, were used on European holidays, Y702 HWT being seen here pausing for a break on the Russian marathon. *Stuart Jones*

Above: For 2002 a new coachbuilder came onto the scene. Spanish builder Sunsundegui was contracted by Volvo to build for the UK, WA taking five. The appearance of Sunsundegui's Sideral was not to everyone's taste, but they were distinctive and reliable. Nice curves, mind. Note WA's bold slogan 'Your local company — Nationwide'. *Stephen Barber collection*

Above and left: The tour operation continued to use a network of interchange facilities. These views at South Mimms Services, at the junction of the M25 and A1(M), feature the reserved area used by the company and a selection of Plaxton and Jonckheere coaches. Note the use of the rear window for advertising — no doubt a contributory factor in the removal of such windows altogether. The Britannia mini-coaches had operated feeders. *Stuart Jones (both)*

Right: A line-up of WA Volvos at South Mimms Interchange in 2003, with a year-old Jonckheere Mistral-bodied B12M nearest the camera. *Stuart Jones*

Left: Volvo B12M/Jonckheere Mistral 'Grand Tourer' GT02 WAP *Lewis Carroll* is boarded by its first passengers. The naming of the Grand Tourer fleet in 2003 proved popular with customers, who often referred to the names in correspondence. *Stuart Jones*

Above and below: Less glamorous were the service vehicles around the interchange network. Leyland National JKH 119L, ex East Yorkshire but new to London Country, and former Leeds City Transport Atlantean/Roe SUG 576M both served as mobile offices and staff mess rooms at South Mimms Interchange. *Stuart Jones*

Above: The introduction of the 'luggage handling' system placed the responsibility for transferring luggage onto the company and not the passenger. To help move the large volume of cases a number of obsolete battery-powered milk floats was purchased, although the height of these vehicles made them less useful than had been hoped. Vehicle LT3, based at South Mimms, is seen loaded with bollards used to block off the WA area of the coach park between interchange times. The attention to detail in the livery is to be commended. *Stuart Jones*

Right: The final flowering? The 'Grand Tourer' concept came late in the company's life but was one of its most popular and profitable ideas, building on a tradition of extra comfort dating back more than 50 years. The original 'Grand Tourers', like Volvo B12M GT03 FFF, seen here on tour in Germany, had Jonckheere Mistral bodies. The final batches were built by Plaxton and were some of the finest vehicles ever to come out of the Scarborough factory. They were a fitting end to a relationship that had endured almost 60 years. *Stephen Barber collection*